INSIDE THE MIND OF ROSE WEST

Also available

Insid the Mind of Jeffrey Dahmer, Christopher Berry-Dee
Inside the Mind of John Wayne Gacy, Brad Hunter
Inside the Mind of the Yorkshire Ripper, Chris Clark and Tim Hicks

INSIDE THE MIND OF
ROSE WEST

TANYA FARBER AND JEREMY DANIEL

G:

Published in 2025
by Gemini Books
Part of Gemini Books Group

Based in Woodbridge and London

Marine House, Tide Mill Way
Woodbridge, Suffolk IP12 1AP
United Kingdom

www.geminbooks.com

Text and Design © 2025 Gemini Books Ltd

ISBN 978-1-80247-268-4

All rights reserved. No part of this publication may be reproduced in
any form or by any means – electronic, mechanical, photocopying,
recording or otherwise – or stored in any retrieval system of any
nature without prior written permission from the copyright-holders.

A CIP catalogue record for this book is available from the British Library.

Printed in the UK
10 9 8 7 6 5 4 3 2 1

Prologue

When Rosemary West stood stony-faced in the courtroom dock, dressed in a dowdy skirt with a blouse and jacket to match, countless lives had been shattered so that her appetite for sadism could be satisfied. Even the biggest media frenzy in decades could not provide enough information for a society searching for more and more details.

The public gaze always intensifies when the murderer in the dock is a woman. Journalists rifle through the archetypes of female killers to find the one that fits best: black widows, femmes fatales, sexy assassins, creepy nurses, baby-faced butchers, sidekicks to sociopathic men. Tabloids chime in with a catalogue of nasty words, and researchers dive deep into the psychology. Tomes will also be written on why women killers fascinate and disgust us in equal measure, shattering the idea that women are, by their nature, nurturers.

But in the case of Rosemary West, there is no blueprint. Even among a tiny portion of killers – women make up only five percent of that population – she is an outlier. A woman of such deep depravity who killed family members and strangers alike seldom comes along, and for that we can be thankful.

PROLOGUE

She had an insatiable lust for inflicting pain on young women and girls, and when she happened to meet Fred West at a bus stop in Cheltenham, the two would soon enter into a pact so macabre that torture, murder, dismemberment and burial under the family home would become the norm.

In the pages of this book, we have tried to explore the mind of, and moments in the life of, a woman who savagely tortured, raped and murdered for her own pleasure, a woman who thought nothing of prowling the streets for a 'plaything' that would later be discarded.

But, in doing so, we have also tried to give the victims and their families what they deserve the most: a dignified portrait of their own lives before Rosemary West and her equally brutal husband intercepted their lives' journeys. Every young woman, girl and unborn child whose lives were taken should be defined by so much more than the horrible end they met at the hands of Rosemary and Fred West.

Sadly, this is not a story of redemption. No heroes arrive at the darkest hour to save the day and right all of the wrongs of the past. There is no moral arc that bends towards justice, and certainly no apologies.

On the day that Rose West finally dies, there will be no deathbed confession or mea culpa.

Her name, next to that of husband Fred, will always be a shorthand for murder most foul, for the embodiment of the worst of humanity. In finding each other, they found unthinkable ways to play out their fantasies, feed their fetishes and treat the victims who crossed their paths as disposable toys.

But while it may not be a story of redemption, it is a story of courage, most notably on the part of their surviving children, some of whom, after a childhood that defies description, went on to become functional adults.

It's an awful tale to tell but it is an important one. When these crimes and the many failures of the systems to protect citizens are documented, we may be a little closer to preventing them from ever happening again.

To this day, there are many unknowns, but there is one thing we know for certain: Rosemary West found a very bad man, made him worse, and discovered in herself the darkest capabilities.

> things are as big as you make them –
> I can fill a whole body,
> a whole day of life,
> with worry
> about a few words
> on one scrap of paper;
> yet, the same evening,
> looking up,
> can frame my fingers
> to fit the sky
> in my cupped hands.
>
> Lucy Partington, 21
> Murdered by Fred and Rosemary West, 27 December 1973

1

A Sugar Sweet Candy-Coated Flossy Merry Time

On 28 November 1953, Daisy Letts stepped through the doors of a psychiatric clinic in the English port town of Bideford, a few miles south of her home in Northam, Devon. Wearing a cheaply made calf-length dress of tweed and pumps with a low block heel and a single strap across the top, she looked no different from other women of the time.

The world was slowly recovering from the devastation of the Second World War, and many families were still dealing with the impact this global conflict had had on mental health, even as glimmers of a better life were beginning to appear. Diagnostics and treatment were, however, a far cry from what they are today, and those who suffered mental ill-health were often shunned or rejected by society.

But for Daisy, it wasn't so much the fallout of a world at war that haunted her mind. Rather, it was the daily battles that played out behind the closed doors of her humble house. It was here where she strained under the burden of caring for four small children, and of her tyrannical husband, Bill, who returned home each evening in a mood that could be sweet or savage.

At a different time, in a different place and with a more bountiful bank balance, she could just as easily have been walking into the warm and nurturing room of a psychotherapist to discuss her harrowing domestic situation. Instead, with the temperature hovering around just 5 degrees, she was about to undergo a procedure that, today, is considered an extreme intervention on the human body.

Daisy had been diagnosed with severe depression, and she was led into a room and onto a bed covered in white linen sheets. As she lay there flat on her back, scared and alone, with a nurse positioning her head correctly on the pillow, the doctor came in holding what might to all the world have looked like a small brown suitcase belonging to a schoolboy.

He opened it up to reveal the latest in groundbreaking medical technology: a small black electrical machine with a few simple knobs, two nodes connected to thin red wires, and, perhaps most absurdly of all, the same dial one would see on a telephone.

With no medication given beforehand to ease the experience, Daisy lay as still as possible while the two nodes were attached to either side of her head and a rubber bite block was placed between her upper and lower her teeth to prevent her from biting her own tongue.

Once she was fully prepared, with the nurse standing at her head to watch over her and hold her chin in place, the doctor turned up the dials, sending an electrical surge through the wires and into Daisy's brain.

As the electrical impulses entered her head, they triggered a series of seizures that lasted up to a minute at a time. Daisy's body stiffened with each impulse, with only small twitches of a few muscles resulting from the experience. But in her brain, where the current was applied, medical experts of the era believed that the chemistry was being altered for the better. When the experience was finally over, the nodes removed from her temples, and her head lying still and heavy once more, the doctor reached for his pen and wrote down in her patient file: 'Electroconvulsive Therapy (ECT) as treatment for Depression.'

So, what was it about Daisy Letts that set her apart from the many other patients that had walked through the doors of the single-storey hospital in Devon that day?

She was just one day away from giving birth to her fifth child, and the small baby girl that exited her body less than 24 hours later was to be named Rosemary Pauline Letts, a person whose gruesome choices and behaviour over the next few decades would stun a nation and shatter the lives of so many people.

***

In Rosemary's case, there were indications that something was wrong from the very beginning. Her mother's words to journalist Howard Sounes on his podcast *Unheard: The Fred and Rose West Tapes* are layered with contradictions and irony that, in light of what happened, seem fitting.

She described Rosemary as a 'model baby' who 'never cried' and 'lay in her pram as good as gold', but also said that 'baby Rose rocked herself so vigorously she would move her pram across the floor'.

The rocking in her pram and cot was a sign that Rosemary was 'troubled' and 'frustrated' and was trying to self-soothe, a behavioural therapist would later say of the behaviour. She said it likely gave Rosemary some sense of 'comfort' as a coping mechanism, and that even as a small baby, she could pick up on the 'disharmony in the home'.

Rosemary would soon have discovered in no uncertain terms, though not fully understood, that her father would also not be a reliable and nurturing caregiver in the absence of a mentally stable mother figure.

Bill Letts, the father of Rose and her four older siblings, had served in the navy during WWII, working on aircraft carriers. In the post-war years, he had struggled to find a steady job. This common post-war slump for males of a certain age was made far worse by his own psychiatric diagnosis: Bill was found to have paranoid schizophrenia as early as his teen years, but with the shameful stigma that this brought, he had kept it a secret as much as possible.

This affliction can lead a person to experience disorganised thoughts, speech, and behaviour. Hallucinations, often in the form of hearing voices, are also common, and it can become increasingly difficult to distinguish between reality and fantasy.

But the main way it presented itself in the case of Bill was that he developed an obsessive-compulsive disorder. In his mind, germs were the sworn enemy to be kept at bay, and he violently enlisted his family members to ensure that happened.

Daisy was so scared of her husband's temper and what he would do if the children came home dirty that eventually she simply forbade them from going outdoors at all.

There is much speculation that it was Bill's behaviour that had caused the long-term depression in his wife Daisy. The post-war years and unemployment would also have played a role, as would the size of the family. Rosemary was already child number five, and two more came along in her wake. A family of nine squashed into small council housing likely raised the temperature in the household.

And so, while it is difficult to finger any factor that shaped the warped mind of Rosemary, the pall of fear and violence that hung over the house, with a delusional Bill holding the strings of that pall, certainly played a part.

The reign of terror that Bill imposed inside the home while being charming and friendly to acquaintances was a blueprint that Rose would later adopt, and to great effect.

***

In 1953, Britain was experiencing a wave of change. In May, the country celebrated the epic achievement of Sir Edmund Hillary becoming the first man to scale Mount Everest; a month later, Queen Elizabeth was crowned in Westminster Abbey, much to the delight of royalists across the land; and while Britain was still living with the effects of the war, food and petrol rationing were lifted.

Suddenly there was a huge influx of cars on the roads, the scarcity mindset of the war years began to fade into memory, and a sense of post-war promise ensued.

But behind the wooden doors of the Letts house in the seaside village of Northam on England's west coast, life did not feel so full of promise. Every indication is that Rosemary's childhood was a joyless one. Deprived of all the common gadgets and activities of a middle-class existence, she never owned a bicycle or learned how to swim. Theirs was not a house where music from a radio set a light mood, and according to Daisy, the family ate meals in total silence as every member strained to decipher Bill's mood, which could turn around and flick to violence any second, especially if he perceived the house as being anything but spotless.

The children were all allocated tasks and beaten if they were not done properly. Alarmingly, Rose and her siblings were forced to clean every square inch of the carpet using toothbrushes. Daisy, far from identifying the extremity of this measure or recognising it as a symptom of her husband's psychiatric condition, obliged and instructed the children to scrub the floors accordingly.

When Rosemary was out of the house and at school, she still had no reprieve from the fallout of her family situation. Her grades were extremely poor, she battled to make even the most tentative friendships, and she was often described as a daydreamer who spent so much time in her 'own world' that she failed to make connections with anyone around her.

At home, she bore witness to all her siblings being savagely beaten by their father, while she was spared this fate. Of course, on the face of it, that seems like a blessing, except it raises the question: was she paying in other ways?

The grim answer to that question is yes. Rosemary was spared the rod because her father had taken to sexually abusing her, and he continued this for several years.

This twisted social dynamic is one that certainly played out in the Letts household. In her book, *Rose West: The Making of a Monster*, criminologist Jane Carter Woodrow writes that Bill 'began sexually grooming Rose but, because this meant she escaped his beatings, she saw it as a warped form of love. By the age of 13, Rose was sexually abusing her two younger brothers too.'

Bill and Daisy slept in separate rooms, and the idea that there was anything sexual going on in her house was allegedly unthinkable to Rose's mother. Speaking to Howard Sounes in the 1990s about those days, she said, 'You think that would have been allowed in our home? Almost impossible. He was so stern. There was nothing sexy in our house. If anything, it was Bill being cruel to them.'

Rosemary, like many children in abusive households, developed the unhealthy coping mechanism of convincing herself it was a happy upbringing. She would later describe her childhood to her solicitor, Leo Goatley, as a 'sugar sweet candy-coated flossy merry time.'

Incest, it appears, had been normalised in her mind, while another unhealthy coping mechanism she developed was repeatedly knocking her head against a wall. Daisy was allegedly aware of this too but sought no expert insight or guidance. She said she thought it was 'just a habit'.

Love, sex and relationships were warped inside the house where Rosemary West grew up, and things were about to get a whole lot worse.

2

Rosemary's Future Husband

When Rosemary was only seven years old, the man she would later join in a twisted spree of torture and murder, Frederick Walter Stephen West, was about to exit his teenage years and experience his first run-in with the law. If Rosemary's homelife was marked by poverty and rationing, the Wests, 150 miles away and also with a mother named Daisy, were experiencing the same.

Fred was born on 29 September 1941 at Bickerton Cottage in Much Marcle, a picturesque village in Herefordshire in the West Midlands surrounded by green countryside and yellow daffodils. At this pivotal moment in British history, with war raging in Europe, these landscapes far beyond the bustle of London's streets had taken on a symbolic role for society as trainloads of children were evacuated from the war-torn capital and perpetual bombing to safer houses in less developed areas. For some children, this journey into the countryside to live with families they'd never met felt like an adventure. For others, it was a confusing social dislocation in which family and neighbourhood life as they knew it was suddenly ruptured. But either way, the green pastures and sparsely populated villages where everybody knew each other by name came to symbolise a quaint and idyllic milieu.

For Fred West's family, however, the Midlands formed a backdrop of hard working-class life that placed them firmly in the role of traditional farm workers – poor but resilient and proud. With a strict and hard-working authoritarian father in Walter West and a devoted and loving mother in Daisy, the West children were imbued with a strong work ethic from an early age. The girls were sent out to pick strawberries during the summer and the boys were taught how to harvest wheat and hunt rabbits. None of this was unusual, and born into such a family in a highly stratified society where your class marks you from birth, Fred West might just as easily have lived the same humble and anonymous life as the tens of thousands around him in that place at that time.

But that's not what happened. Instead, decades later, his legacy would be cemented as one of the most evil killers Britain has ever seen.

***

From the moment his mother held him in her arms, Fred became the apple of her eye, not least because he was the first baby to survive after two siblings had already died during childbirth. Little is known about the impact of these two deaths on his mother, Daisy, but it is unlikely she received any emotional support.

It is also likely that in the 1940s, with thousands of British mothers experiencing the trauma of losing their sons on the battlefields of a global war, Daisy Letts would not have stood out in her community's eyes as someone who had experienced a double tragedy.

This might go some way to explain why, from day one of her first surviving baby's life, Daisy's attachment to Fred was extreme, and it endured after his five siblings, Doug, John, Kitty, Daisy and Gwen, were born.

Fred was a beautiful baby by anyone's standards. With a mass of blonde curls, deep blue eyes and fleshy lips, he was the quintessential cherub-faced infant, and his mother certainly treated him as the angel he appeared to be.

When the six children weren't working out in the field, they were sitting in classrooms at an unremarkable local school. It was here that Fred's status as 'mother's favourite' began to work against him. He showed little interest in scholastic achievement, and though he did better at art and woodwork, he could barely read or write when his classmates were already steaming ahead. But instead of finding ways to bring him up to speed with his schoolwork, his mother blamed the school and made a spectacle of her accusations.

On more than one occasion, she burst through the gates of the school grounds and sought out whichever teachers she felt were responsible for her son's poor grades. He quickly became the butt of jokes from the other children, who laughed at him for being the boy whose overweight, poorly dressed mother turned up at the school to shout at the teachers for picking on her favourite child. It was no surprise to anyone when, at age fifteen, Fred, the boy described by his classmates as scruffy and lethargic, packed his books into his tattered school case for the last time and walked off through the gates of an educational institution for the last time. With no scholastic commitments to take up his day, he simply worked as a farm labourer with not much else going on.

But then, at the age of seventeen, an incident occurred that some say had such an impact on his brain that it changed him irreparably and set into motion the bizarre and destructive behaviour that would shape the rest of his life.

The date was 28 November 1958 as Fred made his way home down a narrow country lane on the 125cc James motorbike that he got on his seventeenth birthday. On this cold winter's day, a young girl called Pat Manns was travelling in the opposite direction on her bicycle. As Fred rounded the corner on the winding lane, he smashed right into her, breaking his arm and leg in the process, splitting his helmet in two and fracturing his skull. His almost-limp body was rushed off to a hospital, where he lay unconscious for an entire week with the distraught Daisy hovering over him around the clock. When he regained consciousness, Fred said that it felt like he was 'coming back from the dead'. The accident was so extreme that some feared Fred would succumb to his injuries – a fate that, in light of the years that followed, would have saved countless families the gut-wrenching heartache that came later.

Instead, he overcame these severe injuries, and it was alleged that from then on, his moods were much darker and he was prone to violent outbursts. His family said he developed 'an extreme fear of hospitals and was prone to fits of rage', and while it is debatable whether this was the start of his strange behaviour or not, the accident had certainly taken its toll on his body. He was left with lifelong facial scarring and a crooked nose that gave his face a more menacing look than before.

It was two years later, at the age of nineteen, that Fred had his first proper run-in with the law.

According to Brian Hill, a friend who was with him at the time, they were in a shop when Fred saw some cigarette cases that he liked and so just took them. Next, they wandered into a jewellery store in the Ledbury high street and started browsing through the various items on display. On the brink of manhood, barely literate, and clearly a farm labourer, Brian likely felt certain he would attract the attention of the staff in a store where more high-end customers were the order of the day. This, however, did not stop Fred from acting swiftly and with ill intent: he had spotted a gold watch that was worth the equivalent of £80 in today's terms, and he simply picked it up, said, 'Christ! That's nice,' and slipped it into his pocket.

The two boys walked out of the store and went to their local pub, The Plough. They hurried into the bathroom near the back, where they hid the watch, plus some stolen cigarette cases, in the cistern of a toilet. The jeweller noticed that the watch was missing soon after the boys left, and he alerted the police about the two rough boys who had been browsing earlier. As they came out of the bathroom, they were met with the image of two burly policemen waiting for them.

They were arrested on the spot, charged with theft, found guilty and told to pay £4 each in fines.

The young Fred, who would later become Rosemary's husband, was emboldened by this experience. Perhaps it made him more brazen to discover that breaking the law ended in nothing much more than a slap on the wrist. Or maybe the thrill of committing a crime and being followed and caught had actually aroused some sensation in him.

Either way, from there things only got worse, making the petty theft of a watch seem like nothing.

***

By the end of 1960, Fred was spending all his spare time at the Ledbury Youth Club. The local hangout had a snooker room at the back, a TV room upstairs and another room with a record player where the locals could sing along and dance to songs like 'Rock Around the Clock' by Bill Haley & His Comets and 'Mack the Knife' by Bobby Darin. The club used to close around 10 p.m., and everyone would then head off to John Jones chippy for a late supper.

One evening, Fred met a dark-haired sixteen-year-old girl with bright eyes and a broad smile. Her name was Catherine Costello, and she was immediately taken with the charming Fred. It wasn't long before the two of them began dating, and given Catherine's own history, she was likely drawn to the excitement of what Fred represented. She too had had her run-ins with the law. Rena, as Catherine was known, was a deft hand at thieving. She had already worked as a prostitute by then, and perhaps saw in Fred the chance of a fun relationship on equal terms. The romance, however, did not last long as Rena moved with her family up to Glasgow in Scotland shortly after the first sparks of the romance were lit. Rena left town, and shortly after her departure, Fred resumed his party-animal lifestyle and any chance to chat up one young woman after the next in the hope of a sexual encounter.

One evening, on the staircase outside the club, Fred thrust his hand under and up the dress of a young woman he was flirting with. She was having none of it and smacked him so hard that he tumbled down the stairs.

With a loud cracking sound, his already-injured head hit hard against the concrete floor. It was so bad that he was knocked unconscious and had to have a steel plate inserted in his skull. Once again, Daisy sat stoically by the bedside of her favourite son, who was unconscious for 24 hours.

When he had finally recovered from the surgery and returned to his work on the farm, fellow farmhands said his behaviour went from bad to worse, with some even referring to him as the one with 'brain damage'.

Up to that point, Fred's problematic behaviour had been dismissed by his parents. Perhaps they simply saw him as a typical teenage boy on the brink of manhood trying his luck with the local girls, or perhaps his father had little connection with him while his mother doted on him and imagined him doing no wrong.

But, in the summer of 1961, when Fred was nineteen years old, that rose-tinted perception of her favourite child would quickly melt away.

His younger sister, also named Catherine but known to everyone as Kitty, was only thirteen years old when she took her mother into her confidence and announced that she was pregnant.

She then broke the horrifying news to her mother: her older brother Fred had been repeatedly raping her for the previous six months.

One might imagine Daisy trying to cover up this horrific act of her darling son, but to her credit, she did no such thing. Fred was swiftly arrested and charged with the crime of 'having unlawful carnal knowledge with a child'.

However, this marked the first of many strange moments in which Fred, caught red-handed, would profess his utter bemusement at the charges levelled against him.

He freely admitted to what he had done and is alleged to have said, 'Doesn't everybody do it?'

It was a big scandal in the village and was soon on everyone's lips. The case came to trial in November 1961, and records show that Fred's mother Daisy was listed as a defence witness. The defence's plan was to argue that Fred's head injuries meant he was not responsible for his actions. But in an unfortunate turn of events, Fred's first charges of sexual assault in the end came to nothing. Kitty's bravery in informing her mother and seeking legal action seemed to melt away. As soon as the case came up in court, Kitty refused to state the name of the man who had abused her. The case was struck from the roll and Kitty watched as her older brother walked off scot-free.

Nobody in the house denied it had happened, though, and the allegations certainly had a chilling effect on Fred's relationship with his family. Daisy was disgusted with her son and kicked him out of the home, and he was forced to move in with his aunt Violet.

It did not take long, however, before the doting Daisy was preparing a bed and hot cup of tea for her eldest son, who arrived on the doorstep with all his bags packed, ready to move back into the family home. It's unclear what happened to the baby that thirteen-year-old Kitty was carrying that had been fathered by her older brother.

***

As fate would have it, Rena had also moved back into the area around this time, returning from Scotland to pick up where she'd left off. The only complication to stand in their way of her resuming a relationship with Fred was the fact that Rena was now six months' pregnant with another man's child.

Seemingly not bothered, 21-year-old Fred and his eighteen-year-old pregnant teenage wife tied the knot. They were married on 17 November 1962 in a hasty ceremony at the Ledbury Register Office, with Fred's brother John as the only family member in attendance. Fred wore a dark, oversized suit and Rena a light blue dress that complemented her platinum blonde hair. The weight of the scandal with Kitty was still fresh in the minds of the townsfolk, and Fred believed his prospects in town were limited, so the newlyweds decided to pack up and relocate eleven days later to the town of Coatbridge in Scotland where Rena had been raised.

Four months later, little Charmaine Carol Mary West was born. In the space where a father's name should have been written on her birth certificate, it was simply left blank.

However, the colour of her skin – darker than your typical Caucasian English child – told a story that her birth certificate covered up. Her father was allegedly a South Asian bus driver, but the story dished out to the conservative folk of an industrial town outside Glasgow was that she was adopted.

Fred also insisted that Rena write a letter to her parents saying that her baby had died in childbirth and that, heartbroken, they had decided to adopt.

While Charmaine was cradled in her mother's arms, Fred set out to look for work and soon found himself employed as a Mr Whippy ice-cream van driver in Glasgow. In some parts of the city in the early sixties, the housing schemes stretched as far as the eye could see, and it was along these nondescript roads that Fred would wind his way with the van.

In order to be nearer this work, the little family packed up their belongings and set off on the ten-mile journey from Coatbridge to their new home in the poorer zones of Glasgow, where Fred soon would get to know every young girl who was on the lookout for a delicious ice cream.

In 1964, Rena fell pregnant with her second child, and by the tender age of nineteen, she had become the mother of two little girls. They named the child Anne Marie. Rena stayed home and looked after her little daughters while Fred went to work, and she was, according to the neighbours, an attentive and competent mother.

However, the man who returned to her each night after his shift was one who had prowled the streets under the guise of his ice cream van, placing him quite neatly in the stereotype of the sinister vendor whose van cruises slowly through the streets playing an eerie version of Greensleeves. If Fred thought he was nourishing his perverse and sordid side under a cloak of anonymity, he was wrong. His behaviour soon drew the attention of the Cumbies, and by all accounts, these Glaswegian gangsters were not people to be trifled with.

The Cumbie gangsters were notorious in the slums of the Gorbals – a district of working-class Glasgow that was replete with overcrowded skyrise buildings and high crime levels. In the decade before Fred West arrived in the area, some 35,000 people were moved from this zone into Castlemilk, where families had more space and cleaner facilities.

It was in this area of Castlemilk that Fred was plying his trade, and though at first he was viewed as a bit of a joke, his roving eye and sleazy behaviour soon became apparent. Many of the families now living in Castlemilk still had strong links with the Gorbals, and on certain days, his route also covered parts of the old slums where the streets still teemed with children sick of the cramped interiors of their houses and flats. They would play football and hide-and-seek, skipping rope and catchers, and so when the ice-cream man came cruising along, they would pull out from their pockets the few coins their parents could spare to purchase an ice cream. It is also alleged that Fred had an affair with a young woman from the slums and impregnated her, but he kept no contact with her or the child, and the relationship, thus falling into obscurity, is hard to prove.

At any rate, his inappropriate way of speaking to the women and girls of the Gorbals and Castlemilk soon caught the attention of the Cumbie gangsters, not least because it was a gang member's fourteen-year-old sister who worked in the van with Fred on the Saturday shift and who told her big brother he had been acting inappropriately.

The Cumbies now had their eye on Fred and were planning to teach him a lesson when a terrible tragedy struck. It was a cold morning in Scotland on the brink of a bitter winter when Fred, allegedly speeding in his van, knocked down a small four-year-old boy named Henry William Feeney, sending his mother screaming into the street to witness her toddler's legs sticking out from under the van.

While in the eyes of the law it was deemed a simple if gruesome accident, this was (and is still not) the belief held by all. As recently as 2018, a writer named Paul Pender, who has interviewed Castlemilk community members who were around at the time of the van accident, said, 'I don't know what the child saw but it was something West would have found compromising if the boy told his mum or dad. Either involving the boy himself or a young woman or girl, who were West's primary targets and victims.'

While it may seem unlikely that a criminal would fear the testimony of a child as young as four, it is possible that Fred's erratic and angry nature could have propelled him to run the boy over deliberately.

Either way, at the time, the Scottish Police released a reserved statement saying that they 'investigate all reports regardless of what time has passed and would encourage anyone who has information to come forward', but the Cumbie gang took the law into their own hands and plotted their revenge against Fred.

As it turned out, however, Fred was able to evade the attack and came to the realisation that it was likely time to leave the area. However, one more strange twist would occur before they packed their bags and left Scotland behind them.

Fred, not surprisingly, had taken to verbally abusing Rena and the children in public. One day, the brazen father and husband was demeaning his wife in front of John McLachlan, a tall and beefy Glaswegian who was not one for taking other people's nonsense. When he stood up to intervene on behalf of Rena and the children, Fred allegedly pulled out a knife. John, however, didn't even flinch. He raised his hands ready for a brawl and Fred could not hold his ground. The knife suddenly meant nothing, and Fred backed down quickly. John was later quoted as saying, 'He wasn't slow in attacking a woman but couldn't tackle a man. It was obvious even then that he was a sadistic bastard who enjoyed beating up women and kids.'

McLachlan told reporter Howard Sounes another ominous story about Fred. Apparently, he rented a garden allotment in the city but he never grew any vegetables there. It was mostly unused soil. McLachlan says that Fred told him, 'I'm keeping it for something special,' and he used to visit it regularly after midnight. Sounes did his research and found out that four young women went missing while Fred was living in Glasgow, but if he was burying his secrets there, then those secrets died with him. A thirteen-lane highway was built that ran right over the area of Fred's allotment.

Fred later discovered Rena was having an affair with John, and as it turns out, this had not taken much sleuth work on Fred's behalf: John had simply 'scratched' out the tattoo of Fred's name on Rena's arm with a sewing needle and replaced it with his own.

Once again, Fred and Rena packed up their lives to look for better prospects elsewhere. Only this time, they were not alone.

3

The Babysitters

By the time Fred West realised it was time to hot-foot it out of Glasgow and back down to the south-west of England, the family configuration had changed somewhat. Along with them, they had his stepdaughter Charmaine, his own baby girl Anne Marie and two young female teenagers who had joined the family.

The first one was Isa McNeill, a sparkly-eyed girl of sixteen with a lyrical voice to match her deep Glaswegian accent. She had been working at Livingstone Industrial Clothing, a knitwear factory mass-producing jumpers and scarves.

She was, however, always on the lookout for new work opportunities, and as was the case with many youngsters in the 1960s when personal freedom was fast becoming the dominant ethos of the age, Isa dreamed of a life beyond the inner-city poverty with which the city had become synonymous.

High-rise blocks had made their mark on the city's skyline the previous decade, with the government opting for a 'villages in the sky' approach in the face of housing shortages that plagued post-war Scotland. Nothing could be more symbolic of Glasgow's economic challenges at this time than these shoddily built high-rises that were so poorly planned, lacked basic amenities, and sprang up on the cheap to house a community that had no other option but to accept what was on offer. This was also an era of mass protests that spread through the streets of Glasgow. The shipbuilding industry was declining at a rapid rate, leaving many Glaswegian families with no breadwinner and dim prospects. Some protested, while others simply went in search of a brighter future if they had the means.

It was against this backdrop that Isa found herself nestled in a chair at a downbeat cafe in Glasgow when she happened to get chatting to a stranger called Rena. So young and with two children constantly hanging off her, Rena spotted an opportunity that could significantly lighten her load: if this young Isa came to work for her and Fred, she could help with the children and provide the kind of conversation and friendship that was sorely lacking from her own husband.

Isa was a Protestant, and despite the religious divides in Glasgow, her best friend since early childhood was a young Catholic girl named Anne McFall. With beautiful dark hair, high cheekbones and her hair cut into bangs across her forehead, the rather naive Anne was also sixteen like her friend Isa and was also eking out her days at Livingstone Industrial Clothing. Anne had likely already seen the dark side of life after spending some of her early years at the notorious Nazareth House in Aberdeen. This home for orphans, like its counterparts in other parts of Scotland, was a site of extreme mental and physical abuse under the guise of religious care.

Not much else is known about Anne's childhood, or Isa's for that matter, but one thing is certain: the girls were looking to break free from the tedium of the clothing factory and the drudgery of Glasgow. There wasn't much money to be made from the nanny work, but for those from broken homes in the poverty-stricken parts of Glasgow, even food and lodging were nothing to be sneezed at.

Anne had also recently lost her boyfriend, who was accidentally electrocuted at work, and had had a terrible fallout with her brother, a notorious gangster. She had done all she could for her severely alcoholic mother, but at the age of sixteen, she was in no shape to be the main caregiver to a parent. She began to spend as much time as she could at the Wests' apartment on Savoy Street in Bridgeton, just east of the city centre, and no doubt sought solace in these newly formed friendships.

After killing the small boy with the ice cream van in November 1965, being hunted down by the Gorbals Cumbie gang, squaring off against Rena's lover John McLachlan, and generally becoming known as someone with an inappropriate eye for young girls and with a sleazy nature to match, Fred decided to leave town before drawing too much heat. It was on 11 December 1965 that he left Scotland, taking the two small children with him and moving back in with the woman who had loomed so large in his childhood: his mother. Back in Herefordshire and looking for work to support his family, Fred picked up a job that would fuel his perverse nature. He was taken into the employ of an abattoir, tasked with driving a van around to collect and transport the corpses of dead animals, while his mother was left to take care of the two little girls.

Daisy made it clear to Fred she had no problem taking care of little Anne Marie and even offered to bring her up as if she were her child rather than grandchild. She was, after all, her flesh and blood and the first offspring of her own favourite son. Where she felt less inclined to help out was with little Charmaine – a spirited child who was not of her blood line and was also mixed race, a definite mark against someone in the racist milieu of the English countryside in the 1960s. This allegedly caused a rift between mother and son, and it did not take long before Fred put in a call to the Herefordshire Children's Department, asking them to collect the one-and-a-half-year-old and two-and-a-half-year-old girls. Upon arrival, the government worker found the two children to be in a pitiable state and whisked them away for safekeeping.

Rena stayed behind in Scotland, with the plan being that she would follow shortly afterwards with Isa as soon as Fred was settled. Anne was then added to the plan too. That the two babysitters would accompany them was likely a mixture of the bonds that had developed, coupled with their belief that the south of England would have a lot more to offer in the way of opportunities than did Glasgow.

Two months later, in the wee hours of 23 February 1966, Fred arrived up north in his abattoir van, which he had not bothered to clean, before ushering Rena into the front and Isa into the back. To Fred's surprise, Anne came walking along too, clutching her meagre belongings before clambering into the back of the van that still reeked of blood and animal innards. After the six-hour drive south from Glasgow to Gloucester, the three young women caught sight of their new home: a brown-and-cream-coloured caravan received in part as payment for Fred's blue Vauxhall.

They also now clapped eyes for the first time on the trailer park where they – this haphazard 'family' – would be living: The Willows caravan site at Sandhurst, Gloucester. It was a place that, at first, had a slight novelty factor for Rena, the babysitters and the two children. This communal living among other trailer park dwellers might have seemed fun for a few days, especially for Isa and Anne, who were up for anything different from the grimness of Glasgow. The toddlers were taken out of social welfare and reinstalled with their mother, father and two babysitter-come-family friends.

But it didn't take long before the three young women realised the trailer home in which they now lived – and the cramped life it represented – was a far cry from what they had hoped for.

The Willows caravan site was on a piece of land that originally formed part of a brickworks. It was only five years before Fred West's arrival that the owner had been granted a licence to allow trailer homes to park on the site at all, and by the time Anne and Isa had moved in with Fred, Rena and the girls, the reality of the lives they would have in England began to dawn on them. Instead of a bustling city with a vibrant nightlife and other job opportunities, the babysitters found themselves squeezed into an unsightly trailer and part of a deeply dysfunctional family of four in the middle of nowhere. If Fred's true colours had already revealed themselves up to now, it was in the confines of the trailer park home that his behaviour deteriorated even further. He became increasingly domineering and aggressive, lauding his power over the women and children. The caravan was also not at all suitable for six people. While he and Rena slept in the tiny room up front, Isa and Anne slept on a small, padded bench in the sitting area, and the little girls on a minuscule pull-out bunk that was to be lifted down from the wall at night.

It was a relief when Fred left for his job each morning, but even so, there was little for the five others to do, especially since Fred had forbidden any trips out to the centre of Gloucester, some twenty minutes away on foot. He had even demanded the little girls' tiny bunk be treated as an enclosure, which they were not allowed to vacate at any time during the day, but the minute he had set off on the muddy paths for the abattoir, the women would lift them down.

By then, Charmaine and Anne Marie – aged three and two – would need much social stimulation, a place to play, and an optimal environment in which to grow. Anne and Isa were still teenagers then and were at an age when one's social life becomes a priority. Rena herself was only 21 and also needed a bigger world than what was on offer at a desolate trailer park among some seventy other trailers in the back of the beyond. The toddlers were frustrated, the teens disappointed by the fallen dreams of moving to England, and Rena was no doubt left wondering how she'd ended up this way, raising two children with a belligerent man who offered nothing by way of love or compassion so early in her life.

When Fred returned from the abattoir each day stinking of meat, he would often beat Rena in front of the children if his dinner wasn't ready. He also felt nothing about hitting Isa or treating the children like they were juvenile delinquents who had to be brought in line. The teens would take the toddlers away to spare them the vision of Rena being beaten, but even little Charmaine got a backhand from her father sometimes, and if her mother tried to protect her, she would get the next round too. He would sometimes even arrive during the day in the van to ensure nobody was disobeying the rules. Curiously at this time, Anne seemed to escape the worst of his wrath, but the reason for this would later become clear.

It's also alleged by neighbours that Fred would go round to their trailer in the evening and, unsolicited, show them pornographic photographs he had taken of naked women and talk about how he was doing backstreet abortions.

With the boredom of the days and fear of the nights stretching ahead of them, the three young women hatched a plan to escape Fred's abuse, take the children with them before it was too late, and have a shot at a better life.

It was at this point that Rena turned to the one man she felt she could trust – the same John McLachlan who had fought for her honour back in Glasgow. As luck would have it, one of his best mates was Isa's boyfriend. His name was John Trotter, and the two young women thus plotted their escape: the two Johns would arrive, overpower Fred if he gave them problems, and whisk the two of them, Anne and the children away to safety.

Knowing Fred's temper and his constant checking up on them, they planned slowly and carefully. It had been six weeks of hell in the trailer, and their lifeline to the outside world was a public telephone that had been installed at the main gate of the caravan park off Sandhurst Lane. If Rena and Isa had first made friends in a cafe in Glasgow, it was now that same setting that could save their lives: Isa snuck off to the public phone one day and took a chance dialling the Victoria Cafe to see if one of the Johns were there. Unfortunately, neither was, but she hurriedly left a message saying McLachlan must ring her back on the public phone at a certain time on a certain day and she'd be sure to answer.

The plan began to take shape. It wasn't long before McLachlan phoned, and on cue, he was incensed by the stories he was told – of Fred's anger and abuse, the cramped conditions, the frustration of the children, the fact that Fred was forcing Rena to earn extra money by pushing her back into prostitution. They agreed on a time when Fred would likely be far out of range, lugging dead carcasses around the country lanes.

It was now almost April, with early signs of spring beginning to show after what had been a bitter winter living in the shadow of the twisted Fred West. It had been Anne's birthday just a few days before, and her solidarity with the other women was on display as they celebrated her special day as well as their imminent escape from life in the trailer park.

On the day of the great escape, Fred went off to work as usual, and a few hours later, the hired car with the two burly Johns inside it came kicking up dust on the lane into the caravan park. The women were relieved and began picking up their bags and could barely contain their excitement to get out of there. But something about Anne's behaviour was off.

It quickly became apparent she was stalling operations and suddenly, the penny dropped.

This young girl, just seventeen, from an appalling background, and with no family members who cared at all where she was, had taken a shine to the manipulative Fred West. Her loyalties now lay with him, to the point that she had tipped him off about the daring escape back to Glasgow, filling in every detail her best friend Isa had shared with her.

Fred arrived back from work unexpectedly, and now an aggressive confrontation ensued among the men, with much screaming from the women. Fred reverted to his usual pattern and began beating Rena, then received a blow to the stomach from John McLachlan. It was at this moment that Anne made her intentions clear: she gathered Anne Marie tightly in her arms and refused to climb into the car. Charmaine, in the meantime, had become like a rope in a tug-of-war between her mother and her stepfather. The more Rena pulled on her to ferry her away to the getaway car, the more Fred West tightened his grip, and the more Isa motioned towards her best friend to take the lifeline of escaping the caravan, the more the vulnerable Anne shook her head and sided with Fred West.

Eventually, Rena and Isa gave up on getting the little girls out, and they escaped with the two Johns, staring out of the window of the car in tears.

Isa remembers Fred threatening Rena, shouting that he 'would kill her if she ever showed her face around these parts again'.

***

Once they were gone and the dust had settled, Fred got back into his work routine, trundling down the streets in his lorry with blood smeared on his clothes and rubber boots. Anne, who had so craved him as a father figure and taken him as a romantic partner, now found herself alone in the caravan looking after the children all day. The sounds of Rena and Isa laughing with her during their hours of freedom and the companionship she felt when Fred was at work were a thing of the past. Instead, she found herself alone with the two small children who relied on her for everything.

But, come nightfall, there was always the romance to look forward to. Later accounts by West himself paint a picture of deep infatuation, them staring lovingly into one another's eyes, and him singing romantic songs to Anne while describing her as his 'angel'. The postcards and letters she sent to her ailing mother were a duplicate picture of this world, but she included a photograph of a large house that she pretended was theirs and which was at least ten times the size of the little caravan. This sad detail is a clear map of what the vulnerable Anne's mind had conjured up – a Cinderella-type marriage fantasy to which she clung and which would ultimately be her downfall.

By the following year (1967), she was heavily pregnant with West's child and was on the brink, or so she might have thought, of becoming the second Mrs West, ready for her happily ever after.

Instead, in the spring of that year, as the days grew warmer and longer, Anne McFall vanished without a trace. No missing persons report was ever filed by the members of her broken family back in Glasgow. Nobody ever came looking for her, not even her old friend Isa, whom she had so badly betrayed by being blinded by her infatuation with Fred West.

Fred simply told others – including Rena, who intermittently returned to the caravan site to see her children – that things hadn't worked out between him and Anne and that she'd returned to her family in Scotland.

She was never seen again – until 27 years later when her body was discovered buried in Fingerpost Field within sight of Fred's parents' cottage.

Her fingers and one of her toes had been cut off, and decaying on top of her own body where her pregnant stomach had once been were the delicate bones of her unborn child.

The young woman Fred West had called his angel, and who had taken a chance on him being the one, became his first known victim.

4

The Early Years

In 1969, at the age of fifteen, Rosemary Letts packed up her meagre belongings and embarked on a new chapter of her life with an older man who she believed would take care of her. The life she was leaving behind had scarred her permanently: a severely depressed mother and an oppressive, paranoid father who made life hell for his children. The family had moved around a lot when Rose was still a child, going wherever Bill could find work, until they finally settled in the picturesque village of Bishops Cleeve, just outside Gloucester.

Her parents split up for a while when she was a young teen, and Rose initially moved in with her mother. But Daisy was still a tormented woman struggling to raise a big brood of children, and soon enough, a decision was made that Rose should live with her father instead.

There are no records of what her life was like when Rose lived alone with her father, but the split between her parents didn't last very long before the family configuration returned to how it had been during her formative years. Family life, such as it was for the Letts family, continued.

Though Daisy didn't know it, this 'family life' she had gone back to included her husband raping their daughter, a young teenager who seemed fascinated by her own developing body, which she would parade around the house naked. Like she had learned from her elders, Rose began molesting her younger brothers during this time.

And so, life in the Letts home was as it had always been. The only difference, as fate would have it, was that they were now living a mere twenty miles away from where Fred West was living when he claimed that Anne McFall had 'returned home to live with her family'.

The Letts's move to the area would set the stage for what was to become one of the biggest and longest serial-killing sprees in the history of the United Kingdom. But for now, it was nothing more than just another change of scenery for a family with sordid secrets behind closed doors, but that looked ordinary to everyone else.

Rose's older sister Glenys had married a man named Jim Tyler, and for a short while Daisy Letts and her children moved in with Jim and Glenys. A small-time entrepreneur, Jim had thought it a potentially lucrative venture to make money off the drivers zig-zagging through the country roads of the Cotswolds. The region, with its rolling hills, emerald meadows, and stone-house villages, had been declared an Area of Outstanding Natural Beauty just two years prior in 1966. It was here where Jim set up his mobile snack bar, which he would park right next to the road, enticing travelling salesmen and truck drivers with a selection of refreshing drinks, chocolates and chips.

Some days were busier than others, but Jim soon realised he could earn what he needed from the mobile snack bar without having to stand there all day, sometimes bored stiff with only a few cars cruising past and even fewer motorists stopping for refreshments. He asked his young sister-in-law, the fifteen-year-old Rosemary, if she would work at the mobile store, and Rose, sensing a pathway out of her oppressive home life, accepted the offer without hesitation. She soon got the hang of the job and began to make full use of the well-oiled bus service that was running in the area and the feeling of independence the new job gave her. What that independence afforded her, her brother-in-law would later claim, was an opportunity for sexual exploits highly unusual for someone her age. Jim would pop by the snack bar only to find it locked. When he looked around for Rose, he often found her inside a vehicle with a customer, usually a stranger she had never met before. And though she never admitted to having sex with the customers, Jim felt certain this was the case.

One day, she was sitting at the bus station in Cheltenham when a man with dark hair and a gap between his teeth came striding towards her. With a great amount of confidence, the man – twelve years her senior – introduced himself as Fred West. Rosemary felt a sense of ill-ease. The man was overbearing and unattractive, but he seemed hellbent on chatting to her. She soon acquiesced and they got into a conversation.

In the days that followed, Rosemary found this self-same man of 27, with his unkempt appearance and shameless manner, waiting for her at the bus stop. He clearly knew what time she caught the bus home, and he made it his business to be waiting there too. At first, his attempts to lure her on a date fell on deaf ears, but after a while, she allowed him to walk her home at the end of the bus ride.

Rose's repulsion had morphed into interest in this older man who had lavished her with such attention, and though she had refused more than once to go on an official date with him, that was all about to change when Fred hatched a plan.

He convinced a woman to walk into the snack bar and tell Rose that there was a man waiting outside to speak to her. As she stepped into the road, there was Fred West again, showing his persistence with a smile on his face.

By this point, it is unlikely Rosemary was aware of the chaos of his personal life, not to mention the fact that he had committed murder in cold blood. During that phase, even as he pursued the teenage Rosemary, Fred, who had moved to a place called Lake House Caravan Site, was constantly splitting up from and getting back together with Rena. The little girls, Charmaine and Anne Marie, were intermittently placed in care, only to return to the caravan once again when Fred and Rena had patched up their rocky relationship. A few days later, they would be removed once again when Rena stormed out and disappeared down the muddy track from the caravan site to the road.

These stories were twisted and used by Fred to lure Rosemary even further into his world. He could now gain sympathy from her by crying foul over Rena's behaviour. He claimed that he was a doting father and stepfather, but that Rena, prone as she was to booze and prostitution, had abandoned him, leaving him to take care of the little girls all on his own. Using lies and flattery, he painted a portrait of himself as a family man who wanted more children and a normal domestic life.

It was on these grounds that Rosemary agreed to offer some assistance while also giving herself an out from the boredom of the snack shop. As the relationship between them strengthened, she said she would help out with the children when Fred was at work.

And that is how Rosemary West, only fifteen years of age, became nanny and later stepmother to two small children, one of whom was her boyfriend's child, and one of whom was his stepchild from a previous relationship.

***

In the autumn of 1969, social services arrived at the caravan and found a young woman looking after the two neglected little girls who had been in and out of care, little Charmaine and her five-year-old sister, Anne Marie. It appeared as if Anne McFall – said to have gone home to Scotland but actually lying buried in a field – had simply been replaced by this new youngster: a teenage girl with dark almond-shaped eyes and a layered pixie cut framing her face.

By then, Rose and Fred were lovers despite her only being fifteen years of age, and with the relationship having become more serious, Rosemary decided it was time to introduce her parents to her new boyfriend.

What Rose perhaps did not predict was their reaction. Her mother, who allegedly knew nothing of the constant rape by her husband of their child, was aghast at the choice of partner her daughter had made. She only thought of her daughter Rose as having grown up in a very strict household, and although Rose had shown signs of heightened sexuality, she had not outwardly shown herself up as someone who would date – and have intercourse with – a man nearing his thirties when she was still a child.

It was at this first meeting when Fred stepped through the doors of the family home that Rose announced she had stopped working for Jim at the snack bar and was taking care of her new boyfriend's two little children instead to earn some money. This 'new boyfriend' also had a motorbike, a home of his own (albeit a small caravan in a country caravan park) and a full-time job at an abattoir, where he would have become used to stunning and killing livestock by using a bolt gun or slitting their throats and dismembering the carcasses by making precise cuts to separate the meat, fat, and bones.

This news was a lot for Rose's parents to take in. Bill, Rose's father, also sensed something dangerous about Fred. He later said to Daisy that he sensed in Fred a man who lies, exaggerates and boasts, and who has an air of violence around him.

At the same time, given Bill's own history of repeatedly raping his daughter, there was likely a heavyweight bout of twisted jealousy in the equation too, and perhaps Rose picked up on this. Bill was, after all, the man who had not only violated her since she was little but had also ruled the house with an iron fist, making someone like Fred appear as an expression of Rose's own freedom of choice. This first meeting between Bill and Fred also came on the back of Jim's reports to Bill of his daughter's behaviour at the snack bar.

After this first encounter with the Letts parents, Fred picked up his motorbike helmet, probably unaware of the terrible impression he'd made, and headed off from the family home. The minute he was out of sight and the roar of his bike's engine was no longer audible, Bill wasted no time telling Rose his thoughts or intentions.

He told her plain and simple: he would not hesitate to call social services if Rose ever saw that man again.

***

If only Rose had heeded the warning. Many shattered lives might not have followed in the wake of this fateful meeting.

But she did not. The allure of Fred West had proven irresistible, and just two months shy of Rose's sixteenth birthday, her father went ahead with his threat. He dialled the number and told the woman on the other end of the phone at social services that his daughter, still a child, had got herself tangled up in an inappropriate sexual relationship with a manipulative older man.

On cue, Rose was whisked away to a so-called home for troubled teenagers. Monday through to Friday each week was a slog. With children from difficult backgrounds all institutionalised together, the place was hardly a soft cocoon. Rose found herself among youngsters who had seen their fair share of hardship, some of whom had developed callous ways to make sense of the world around them.

At dusk each Friday, many of these youngsters would return for the weekend to the broken families from which they had come. Those running the place imagined young Rose doing just that: heading off with a small suitcase to her parents' and siblings' house in Bishops Cleeve. What they didn't know was that, in reality, she was heading straight into the arms of her older lover in his brown-and-cream caravan parked in the middle of a campsite. What Rose didn't know was that her predecessor had been murdered. So here she was, from Friday to Sunday, playing the role of the new girlfriend and stepmother before heading back to the institution to carry on the charade of 'healing' for another week.

But this configuration did not last long. On the technicality of her age, Rose simply bided her time until the morning of her sixteenth birthday, when she was legally free to make her own choices about her living arrangements. Without a second thought, she packed up her small case of clothes at the institution, headed off to the family home once more to pick up the rest of her belongings, and made a beeline for the caravan park.

The shock in that moment was written on Daisy's face. She later recalled that her sister (Rose's aunt) had been visiting that day when Rose came home to pack her bags. The aunt had sat transfixed as her niece, raised in this family of oppression where the father called every shot, simply stuffed her goods into a bag and, without a trace of sentimentality, moved out and off to chart her own course. On discovering what was happening, Bill, somewhat predictably, bellowed and raged around the house, scaring the bejesus out of his wife and his other children as he had always done before. But where before he could evoke the threat of social services, he now had no legal backing in his arsenal.

And just like that, Rosemary Letts had escaped the clutches of her obsessive-compulsive father, whose personality had cast a long shadow over the family home for more than a decade.

But now came another twist. Waiting in the caravan park for Rose was an empty caravan. Fred, as it turned out, was in jail serving a thirty-day sentence for theft and unpaid fines. The children were in foster care – again – and however warped Bill Letts's own behaviour had been, he was not wrong to worry about the man into whose arms his daughter was escaping. On the surface, he was a petty thief. In reality, he was a murderer. But for Rose Letts, nothing mattered other than waiting patiently for her boyfriend to come home.

And come home he did. When his sentence was up, he came cruising down the path of the caravan site, seemingly without a care in the world, to where Rose was waiting for him. With the girls in foster care, the two spent their first evening alone together, sleeping in the same caravan bed that Fred had once shared with Rena and then Anna.

This arrangement soon morphed into the dream of living like a 'normal' family. Fred and Rose scoured the local classifieds and eventually found a small flat in Gloucester, that they decided to call home. They picked up Charmaine and Anne Marie, and kitted out the humble abode as best they could.

Bill, meantime, could still not accept the choice his favourite child had made. In early 1970, less than a year after his first tense meeting with Fred at the family home, he dragged Rose off to the police station. Once again, and this time with the help of a police officer, he tried to convince his daughter to come home. He told her, in the presence of the police, that Fred was a dangerous person who did not have her best interests at heart.

This time around, of course, Bill knew that the authorities could not step in. On the technicality of her age, she was a free agent to decide her own living conditions. However, the police still had one trick up their sleeve: to share Fred's criminal record with the young Rose in the hope that, like any normal person, she would see that giving him a wide berth was her best option.

She already knew he had committed crimes, though, and wouldn't budge. Also, in light of what the future held, his criminal activities could have been a spark that ignited Rose's attraction even further.

***

Around that time, another piece of shocking news landed.

Rose was pregnant with Fred's baby. This older man she'd met at a bus stop rather recently, who had then shamelessly pursued her, hired her as a nanny and finally seduced her, was now to be the father of her child. One can only imagine the horror in Bill and Daisy's minds: their teenage daughter, still a child herself just a few months prior, would soon be nursing a newborn with two other young children also needing care.

Once again, the family decided they needed a new home, so they moved to a flat in Midland Road, Gloucester, but it was better suited to their needs than the small place they had just left in Cheltenham.

When the day of the birth arrived, the couple named the new little girl Heather, and Rose and Fred were, on paper, to begin the journey of raising her together.

But, just two months later, Fred was arrested. He had stolen the tyres off a car, and the police had enough evidence to prove it. Once again, he was carted off to the local prison, and this time, with not two but three children to take care of, Rose found herself in a situation for which she was truly unsuitable. On bad terms with her family, she also had none of the help that an extended family might offer, and other than the odd visit from her one brother who would arrive with a small bag of food, she was alone with the children.

It was around this time that she also began prostituting herself, with a steady stream of men now entering and exiting the house in full view of the children.

It was also against this backdrop that the violent and abusive side of her personality emerged from the shadows, although it is of course possible she had already displayed signs of it when she had looked after Charmaine and Anne Marie before Heather was born.

According to neighbours, Anne Marie was a quiet and subservient child who tried to fade into the background, particularly in the presence of her young stepmother. Charmaine, on the other hand, who was now eight years of age and was neither Rose nor Fred's own child, stood up to Rose.

There is a record of a trip to a local hospital that gives clues to this time in Rose's journey to committing murder: she took Charmaine to an emergency clinic because of a large puncture wound in her ankle. While she made up a story to explain it, there was major speculation she had inflicted the wound herself, and she allegedly made several visits to different hospitals so that nobody was able to join the dots of her abuse towards Charmaine.

In one of the flats next door to the home in Midland Road, Gloucester, there was a little girl named Tracey Giles. Years later, she described a chilling scene that made perfect sense in light of the gruesome crimes that Rose and Fred went on to commit: Tracey's mother had run out of milk and asked the little girl to pop by the Wests' house to borrow a pint. The door was unlocked – not uncommon at the time – and she entered the home unannounced.

There before her was a scene she would never forget: Charmaine was standing on a chair with her small hands bound tightly behind her back with a belt. Rose loomed over her with a large wooden spoon she had clearly been using to strike the child.

Tracey later described to her mother what she had seen and added the most worrying bit of all – that Charmaine was not reacting at all. She was standing on the chair as if this was a common and 'ordinary' part of her everyday life. Anne Marie stood in the doorway when it happened, with a lost expression that seemed to indicate she had disassociated from what was going on in front of her eyes, or was also seemingly unperturbed as if this was normal life. Tracey told her mother that Rose said Charmaine had to be punished because she had been mischievous. Charmaine had told Tracey on many occasions that, unlike her sister, who was Fred's own child, she could stand up to Rose because any day now, her real mother (Rena) was going to come and get her and save her from Rose's beatings.

As it turned out, however, by the time Rena returned, it was too late.

The timeline is unclear, but the records show that on a warm and mild Tuesday morning, 15 June 1971, Rosemary gathered up the two young sisters and the eight-month-old Heather and headed to the local prison to visit Fred.

While Fred was locked up in 1971, Rose wrote him a note which only emerged decades later during the trial. 'Darling, about Char,' the note read. 'I think she likes to be handled rough. But darling, why do I have to be the one to do it. I would keep her for her own sake, if it wasn't for the rest of the children.'

The cryptic nature of the note makes it hard to parse exactly what Rose was saying, but in some lights, it looks like a stunning admission that they were already engaged in a conversation about getting rid of Charmaine and that it was only a question of who and when the murder was going to happen.

In any event, that visit to see Fred in prison was the last time anyone ever saw Charmaine West alive.

Fred was released from prison nine days later, and thus began Rose and Fred's fabrication of what had happened to the little girl. Rose walked down to the local school, where she told the staff that Charmaine had been sent off to London to take up a great opportunity at a city-based school.

Anne Marie, Charmaine's quiet sister who had borne witness to far more than anyone her age should ever see, was told that her older sister had travelled to Scotland to live with Rena, the girls' mother.

And so, over the course of the next two months, Rose and Fred's dark secret of Charmaine's fate did not raise any further suspicion among those in their immediate surroundings. But, of course, her mother Rena had started worrying about her daughter. Ever since Rena's dramatic departure with McLachlan from the caravan site a few years prior, she had appeared on and off wherever Fred was living to check up on the children who had been in and out of social service care more times than anyone could count. Since Rose moved in, they had not been in care outside the home, and though Rena's life had been marked by alcohol and prostitution, she had never stopped contacting her daughters by phoning for a chat to check up on them.

By August 1971, she was worried sick. She had not spoken to little Charmaine in two months and Fred was not giving a straight answer as to why this was the case. Rena was still terrified of Fred, scarred by the memories of the frequent beatings she had endured behind the closed doors of the caravan, but for the sake of her children, she knew she had to make the journey from Glasgow to Gloucester to find out why Charmaine was never available for a chat on the phone, and possibly to take her back to Glasgow.

Rose was allegedly at home without Fred when there was a knock on the door. She opened it to find Rena standing there, asking where Charmaine was. Rose made an excuse, and the two women waited for Fred to return home. When he did, he allegedly reassured her once again that Charmaine was fine and would be home soon. He suggested they head down to the pub while they waited.

According to the records, Fred plied Rena with alcohol until she was paralytically drunk. He then led her to a car, draping her floppy arm around his neck for support, and installed her on the passenger's seat. Within seconds, she had passed out.

Fred now drove out of town towards his former home on the Gloucestershire-Herefordshire border. He stopped the car and placed his hands around the neck of his first wife and squeezed as hard as she could until she stopped breathing.

Rena, 26, who had asked too many questions about the whereabouts of her daughter, had now been silenced permanently. It had been four years since Anne McFall, Fred's one-time girlfriend and eighteen-year-old mother of his unborn child, had been murdered by him and buried in a grave in Fingerpost Field near Much Marcle, not far from his family home.

Fred now took it upon himself to cut Rena's lifeless body into small pieces, which he placed inside plastic bags. The woman he'd once been madly in love with, whom he had married despite her pregnancy by another man and who was the mother of his own child, was now dead. Her mutilated body was treated as nothing more than a secret that had to be hidden, and that is exactly what Fred did.

He dug a grave close to a clump of trees in Letterbox Field near Much Marcle and placed the plastic bags inside, covered it up and began the drive home to Midland Road.

Rena and Anne, who had once been close friends but who had fallen out when Anne betrayed Rena by tipping Fred off about the daring escape from the caravan site, now lay in graves not far from each other, and would remain there, undiscovered, for the next two decades.

***

But what about little Charmaine? What had happened to the feisty and rebellious little girl whose death Fred was trying to conceal by killing her mother who had come looking for her?

The two stories that later emerged stand in direct contradiction to one another, but both end in the same place – with Charmaine having been brutally murdered in the summer of 1971.

In one version of events, Rose acted alone when she killed Charmaine, just before Fred's release from his ten-month stint in the local prison. In this version, Fred, on his release, did Rose's bidding by digging a grave below the kitchen window at the Midland Road house before cutting Charmaine's body into small pieces and then burying her there. Nobody suspected a thing at the time, though Rose's brother George later recalled an incident when Fred threatened him and beat him for wandering into the kitchen unsupervised.

Charmaine's body remained undiscovered until 1994, and that same year, when the story of Rose and Fred West truly came to light, Fred claimed Charmaine had been asleep in the back of the car when he strangled her mother Rena to death and that he had then killed her too to cover his tracks.

He claimed that he wrapped the child's body up in a blanket and drove it back to the Midland Road home, where he hid it in the basement area until he was able to bury it. He also claimed that in later years, when he returned to the house to build an extension for the owner, he dug up her remains and put them even further down in the foundations 'to make sure of it'.

Fred was a pathological liar, and it is likely that this story, like many of his others, was a fabrication told in a futile attempt to shield Rose from taking the blame. But the evidence points more to Rose having committed her first murder alone when she took the life of Charmaine West. The coroner on the case more than two decades later pinpointed June rather than August as the month during which Charmaine had been murdered.

Another disturbing fact is that when the post-mortem was done on Charmaine's body 23 years after her death, it looked as if the body had been severed at the hip. Fred consistently maintained he would not have dismembered his own daughter and that the damage must have happened during the later building work he conducted at the property in 1976. However, several bones – particularly the kneecap, finger, wrist, toe and ankle bones – were missing from Charmaine's skeleton, leading to the speculation that the missing parts had been retained as keepsakes.

To this day, the exact circumstances of Charmaine's death at age eight remain unclear, but one truth persists: her murder marks a grotesque turning point in the story, one in which two warped minds collaborated in treating the dead body of an innocent victim as inconvenient evidence that should be erased off the face of the earth.

5

Caroline – The One Who Got Away

Around the time of Charmaine's death, followed closely by that of her mother who had been desperate to find her but ended up dead and buried in a field near Fred West's childhood home, Rosemary knocked on the door of her parents' home. The teen mother, who had walked out so defiantly with her bags just a few months before, now said what her father had wanted to hear all along: that she had misgivings about the road she had chosen to travel with the older man she'd met at a bus stop. She watched the relief spread across her mother's face when she informed her parents that she had decided to leave Fred West forever. She explained that she'd had enough with the way things were between them and that she was moving out. But no sooner had those words left her mouth when another knock came at the door. This time it was Fred, and he was looking to reclaim his wife.

Daisy later would recall a scene where Rose was standing between her father and her fiancé. She turned to Bill and told him in no uncertain terms, 'You don't know him. There's nothing he wouldn't do … including murder.' But Fred knew how to reach Rose in ways that her parents never did, and he simply ignored what she was saying and spoke passionately until her resolve began to weaken, not least by the teenager hearing the words that confirmed their special bond, 'Come on, Rosie, you know what we've got between us.'

While just a few minutes before she was telling her father that Fred was capable of murder, she now took his hand and exited the family home once again, heading for the flat in Midland Road, Gloucester, in order to continue building a life together – and, as it turns out, taking the lives of others over and over again.

***

While the city of Gloucester had a long and storied history as an elegant cathedral city, by the 1970s it had developed into a gritty, working-class industrial centre of England. The local economy was heavily reliant on traditional engineering and manufacturing, with major employers like the Gloucester Railway Carriage and Wagon Company, Fielding & Platt and the Gloster Aircraft Company that offered rough men like Fred plenty of work when times were good and a very thin safety net when the tide turned.

As the character of the British economy changed during that decade, the industrial sectors, and hence the city itself, began a steep decline. The depressing, tough character of Gloucester that had emerged in the post-war era was reinforced by recession, rising unemployment and economic stagnation as the manufacturing base contracted.

But economic concerns and their diminishing prospects were far from their minds when, on the cold and grey morning of 29 January 1972, Rosemary took her lover's hand in the banal setting of a registry office, where they signed on the dotted line as the newly betrothed Mr and Mrs West. The only other person present at the wedding was Fred's brother John. Nobody from the large Letts family was invited, and it's unclear if they knew that it was happening or if they would have had any desire to witness this union.

At the time of their marriage, Anne Marie was just shy of turning eight, and little Heather was only fifteen months old. Their guardians, Fred and Rose, between them, though not together, had already murdered three people. But far from taking stock of their lives or needing to evade police or run from the law, they were able to simply carry on as if they were an average young family marking each milestone on a normal course of events.

Inside Rosemary's womb at the registry office was the next child: a girl who would be called Mae June, so named because her birth on 1 June 1972 coincided with the changing of the month. It was also around this time that they packed up their belongings and closed the door for the last time on the two-storey Midland Road house. The new tenants moved in shortly after they left, with no idea of the dark union that the place had housed. The young couple's ghastly, bloody secrets would stay hidden from the world, just as the remains of little Charmaine would remain buried under the Midland Road house with nobody coming to look for her in her mother's wake.

Anne Marie, for her part, must have pined for her feisty older sister and wondered why her real mother had never come to check up on her again or been on the other end of the phone. She, too, walked out of the house for one last time, with nobody on her side to protect her from the horrors that would soon follow.

Now the newlyweds unlocked the door to the place they could truly call their own and where they would live for the rest of their lives until their arrest. The new house that they found was only half a mile away from Midland Road, a short walk up past the War Memorial and around the serenity of Gloucester Park.

Initially, the three-storey home at 25 Cromwell Street was rented from the city council, but it wasn't long before Fred purchased the property from the council for £7,000, which was the equivalent of around £120,000 in today's terms. A narrow three-storey semi-detached, it was the last in a row of many identical such houses, with a very plain facade, beautified only slightly by embellishments above a single narrow window on each of the storeys. Because it was the last in the row, it also had a single window on the flank and a squat neighbouring building that wasn't constructed from the same mould: a bland single-storey church for the Seventh-day Adventist congregation with a cross made of glass bricks cemented into its front.

The house was set up so that the sexual services at 25 Cromwell Street all happened in a room on the third floor that had a sign hanging on the door that said 'Mandy's Room'. Rose carried the only key to this room on a string around her neck, and Fred installed a separate doorbell to the household, which her clients were instructed to ring whenever they visited and which only Rose would answer. Fred built a private bar in Mandy's room and set up a red light outside the door to indicate when Rose was working and not to be disturbed. As soon as the renovations were complete, Rose began advertising her services as a prostitute in a local classified magazine under the name Mandy. Whether he thought it was a way for her to operate incognito or because he liked the idea of his wife being with men of other races, Fred encouraged Rose to seek clients from Gloucester's West Indian community through her personal ads.

A lodger called Elizabeth Brewer recalls Rose saying that after she retired, she would just have sex all the time. She ran brazen ads in local magazines, advertising her services, one of which read: 'Sexy housewife needs it deep and hard from VWE (very well endowed) male, while husband watches – coloureds allowed'. She was allegedly notorious in Cromwell Street for throwing open the windows and making a lot of noise while having sex so that the whole street could hear what was going on.

The third income stream from the lodgers came at an initial cost: Fred put their hard-earned money into converting the rooms on the upper floors into bedsits, and he made sure to install a cooker and washbasin on the first-floor landing. This would ensure that the lodgers, forbidden from using the small garden at the back of the property, would also have no cause to enter the ground floor where Rosemary and Fred lived with the children. Fred's handyman activities in the house also extended to a bizarre Hawaiian-style beach bar that he constructed in the living room, which provided a macabre, festive atmosphere amongst all of this chaos and depravity.

The family of five, on paper, were like any other family in the area: making ends meet as best they could, going about their daily lives, and coming and going from their semi-detached just as any other neighbour. They were, as far as anyone could see, a 'normal' family, driving around in their grey Ford Popular, the cheapest entry-level car in the UK at the time but nonetheless a step up from Fred's motorbike and the abattoir van that had so repulsed Anne McFall and Rena on their trip down from Scotland. Appearances are often deceiving.

Any loyal readers of the *Gloucester Times* who opened the paper on 13 January 1973 would have been met with a harrowing story, which read as follows: 'A 17-year-old was stripped, bound, gagged and sexually assaulted by a married couple, the Gloucester City Magistrates heard yesterday. The couple, 31-year-old Fred West and his 19-year-old wife

Rosemary admitted to assaulting the girl causing actual bodily harm. They also pleaded guilty to indecently assaulting her.'

***

The 'girl' in this disturbing newspaper article was named Caroline Owens. With a short, feathered fringe, high cheekbones, neat eyebrows and dark silky hair, she had just the face for modelling in the early seventies; though she showed promise doing this on an amateur basis, it was hardly a lucrative or full-time job.

Caroline lived in Gloucester, and one of her greatest delights was travelling a little way up north to visit her boyfriend. He lived in Tewkesbury, ten miles along the M5, and with no transport of her own, Caroline would not think twice about sticking out her thumb and jumping into a stranger's car.

One early evening, as she stood on the side of the M5, a grey two-door Ford Popular pulled onto the shoulder of the road. Caroline, relieved at having nabbed a lift, waited while the young woman in the passenger seat climbed out and ushered her onto the backseat.

She said her name was Rose. The man, who introduced himself as Fred, said they were more than happy to drop Caroline where she needed to go, despite the fact that it was not en route. On this particular night, Caroline was actually headed towards her mother, who lived near the Forest of Dean, rather than her boyfriend up north. By then, hitching was second nature to Caroline, and she thought nothing of the bespectacled young mother and her older husband who pulled up on the side of the road and offered her a lift.

As with all her previous rides, Caroline got chatting to the couple that had been kind enough to stop for her. They set off down the highway making polite conversation, with the married couple peppering the young hitcher with questions about herself and listening attentively to her answers.

After the twenty-mile ride, it was time to say goodbye. Rose, still pregnant with Mae at the time, climbed out to release Caroline from the back seat. She thanked them for the lift, and just before the girl walked off, Rose stopped her and said they would love to employ her as a nanny. She explained that with one small girl, a toddler, and another baby on the way, the Wests could do with all the help they could get. Free lodging and £3 a week were hers if she wanted the job. Caroline thanked them, declined to take up the offer on the spot, but promised she would consider it.

A few days later, Rose was at home when there was a knock on the door. She opened it to find the young hitcher from a few days earlier. Caroline asked Rose if the offer still stood, and Rose said of course, that she and her little family would love to bring Caroline into the fold at Cromwell Street.

Rose stood back and held the door open as Caroline entered the house. She then led Caroline to the room where she would be staying. It was small, sparse and simple, and Caroline was taken aback to find she wouldn't have the room to herself. She would be sharing it with their daughter, a shy and overweight eight-year-old who spoke in a soft voice and said her name was Anne Marie.

Rose was only two years older than Caroline, and soon enough, a friendship started to develop between them. The two young women got along very well, and it was because of this closeness that Caroline took it as 'matter-of-fact' when Rose would stroke her dark hair and comment on how lovely it was. She would also tell Caroline she had beautiful eyes. Caroline would later describe Rose as having a 'whiny, drippy' voice, until she'd begin screeching at the children. That was when her darker side would be more obvious, as she'd fly into an explosive rage at the slightest provocation and then yell her lungs out at the little girls.

Fred, for his part, would get home from his long working days and start talking nonstop while he sat down to eat his supper. She was just a few days into her new job as a nanny when Caroline began to notice the red flags about her employers and landlords.

Caroline would later recall Fred's strange demeanour and how the things that he said made her feel deeply uncomfortable. He spoke incessantly about his favourite topic – sex. He would also consistently grope Rose no matter who else was around, putting his hand up her skirt while she was cooking or fondling her breasts over her shirt in full view of Caroline and the children. Disturbingly for young Caroline, there were always sex toys and pornographic publications lying casually around the house, and Fred would always boast about being 'God's gift to women'.

Caroline found this odd since what she saw before her, she would later recall, was a 'short little man with piercing blue eyes, a flat, wonky nose and thick lips that hid a gap in his front teeth'.

Beyond Fred and his obvious appetites, there was a steady stream of men who arrived at the house any time of day or night to be led up to the third floor and into the private room that nobody else was permitted to enter. To satisfy his insatiable desires and voyeurism, Fred had drilled various peepholes into the walls that provided a view into Mandy's room. He had also installed a baby monitor in the room, allowing him to listen to what was going on from elsewhere in the house. If Fred could hear it, then no doubt so could the children and so could Caroline.

Already unnerved by the hypersexual atmosphere in the household, Caroline was even more taken aback when, one evening, Rose and Fred invited her into the living room and asked her to consider joining them for group sex with a few other people they regularly met with.

Another red flag was raised when Fred told Caroline not to worry about falling pregnant because he could help perform a termination of pregnancy on her.

And yet, the most disturbing thing of all was still to come. One day, Caroline and Anne Marie were sitting in a room together chatting when Fred arrived unannounced. He nodded towards his eight-year-old daughter and proudly told Caroline that his daughter of eight was no longer a virgin. Caroline, obviously shocked at this, turned to the little girl to whom she was a nanny and roommate. Anne Marie cast her eyes to the ground and hung her head in shame, and Caroline realised with a start that Fred was telling the absolute truth.

At seventeen and with her own self-protection instincts finally kicking in, Caroline did not probe this situation any further. This was the final warning that she needed, and the only thing she could think was to get out of 25 Cromwell Street as quickly as possible. She packed her clothes into her suitcase, gave Anne Marie a hug goodbye, and announced to Rose and Fred that she could no longer work for them. She was relieved when they made no attempts to stop her.

That was the last time she expected to see them, and she soon returned to life as she had known it, freed from her role as the nanny in a home where things had gone so completely wrong.

***

A few weeks later, on a particularly cold evening, Caroline stood on the side of the road with her thumb out once again. History seemed to be repeating itself. The grey Ford Popular pulled onto the shoulder of the road, and there inside sat Rose and Fred West. Caroline felt no sense of threat as Fred turned on the charm and told her there were no hard feelings and that they were more than happy to assist with a lift. Once again, Rose climbed out of the vehicle so Caroline could get in, and off they drove into the night.

Caroline settled onto the back seat, expecting to be at her destination within half an hour, but then things took a sinister turn.

On a quiet section of country road, Fred pulled the car over and turned the lights and the ignition off. In the pitch dark, Rose climbed onto the back seat. She slung her arm around the teenager's neck, and Caroline suddenly felt Rose's cold hands fondling her breast. Caroline protested and tried to remove her arm when suddenly, out of nowhere in the inky darkness, she felt Fred's hard fist punching her in the face. He did this several times until Caroline blacked out.

Without knowing how much time had passed, she eventually came to and tried to get her bearings. She was still in the Wests' car, but now her hands were tied tightly behind her back and a scarf had been stuffed into her mouth and secured with sticky tape. All she could do was breathe through her nose and sit in terrified silence as the car wove its way through the darkness all the way back to 25 Cromwell Street.

The inside of this house she knew so well was deathly quiet. If Anne Marie was awake, she knew better than to make a sound. Caroline tried to call for help but this only infuriated Rose, who grabbed a pillow and held it over Caroline's face to smother her cries. Fred then entered the room and Rose told him that the girl had been trying to call for help. Fred then grabbed her by the throat and threatened, 'I will take you to the cellar where our black friends will be allowed to use you.'

Caroline's nightmare was only beginning.

Rose and Fred ripped her clothes off and pushed her down onto a dirty mattress on the floor before tying her arms together. From there, the sexual violence began, with Rose and Fred beating and sexually abusing her while the children slept.

Caroline would later recall how Rose grabbed her hair and yanked the teenager towards her, swearing as she did. Rose and Fred then spoke over each other, calling Caroline different names and clearly deriving pleasure from doing so. She was certain that they were going to kill her as the abuse went on throughout the night and lasted some twelve hours.

Caroline was not surprised that this was who Fred really was, but she was most shocked at Rose's behaviour. She had considered Rose a friend in the sense that they had been close while she was living there and of similar ages, but also as a mum, since she was the woman of the household and the mother of the children Caroline had once looked after.

This deep sense of betrayal only underscored what was already a horrific experience unfolding, punctuated by Fred adding these words to the other insults and threats: 'When we've finished with you, we're going to kill you and bury you under the paving stones of Gloucester.'

In his usual boastful and over-the-top manner, he claimed there were already hundreds of girls buried there, and he seemed to take as much pleasure in Caroline's fear as he did in his own sexual gratification. Eventually, Rose and Fred had tired themselves out and now fell asleep on the same mattress where Caroline still lay bound and naked, but eventually she passed out too.

When morning broke, Rosemary finally left the room and Caroline thought the abuse was over. She was wrong. With Rose gone, Fred pounced on Caroline and raped her before bursting into tears and asking her to not tell Rose what he had done.

Caroline later said she believed Fred was crying not because he was sorry about what he had done, but because he was scared that Rose would find out and would be angry with him. He offered her a bath and tried to be nice to her.

Caroline's survival instinct kicked in and she managed to convince the couple that she was not too upset by what had happened and that she would return to work for them again. She knew this tactic was her best chance at getting out of 25 Cromwell Street alive.

After the bath, the three of them climbed back into the Ford Popular, where the nightmare had begun the evening before, and drove off to the laundromat as if it were a normal day of domesticity. In the first bit of luck she had had, the streets of Gloucester were teeming with cars and Fred could not find a parking spot, so he dropped the two women off outside the laundromat and said he'd keep looking for a spot. Now Caroline saw her chance. She said goodbye to Rose in a very calm manner and told her she would see her for work the following day. Caroline darted off in the opposite direction before Rose had time to assess the situation or protest. She only wanted one person in the whole world: her mother.

When the young woman arrived back at her home, patches of black and blue bruising had come up all over her body from the horrific ordeal the night before. Her mother was stunned and outraged. It took a great amount of courage for a seventeen-year-old girl to report rape and assault by a couple that had threatened to kill her and knew where she lived, but Caroline agreed to be escorted to the local police station by her mother to report the crimes committed against her by Rose and Fred West. The very least she expected was for the police to be on her side. But, as it turns out, that wasn't what happened.

The detective that was brought in was not only devoid of compassion but also went about victim-blaming the highly traumatised Caroline. She had only escaped her attackers a few hours earlier, and now she had a policeman accusing her of being promiscuous and being 'up for it'.

At the very least, a case was opened. Unsurprisingly, when the Wests were told that they had been accused of serious crimes, they denied it. It was the narrative of two adults and parents versus that of a teenage girl, and they were confident they would be believed. After some negotiation in the magistrates' court, Fred and Rose agreed to plead guilty to a lesser charge of assault in exchange for all the other charges being dropped.

In later years, Caroline told the *Independent* newspaper that there were a number of reasons for not pursuing the rape charge. 'I'd had an affair with one of the lodgers at the house, and another had tried to sleep with me. The Wests had told the police about this and I was terrified of people finding out. And my stepfather, with whom I had a difficult relationship at the time, didn't want me to go to court as he was worried about neighbours gossiping.'

Despite the horrific nature of the attack, the Wests were only fined a paltry £50 each, and to add insult to injury, the magistrate proclaimed he believed it would not be in the Wests' 'best interests' to send them to prison. Had he acted differently, many other lives might have been saved. Why? Because Rosemary West and her twisted husband had learned one dark lesson from this episode: letting a victim get away after a night of sexual violations was way too dangerous, and they would never make that same mistake again.

6

Three Young Women, No Police Suspicion

In 1973, the average age of first-time mothers in the United Kingdom was around 25 years of age. That same year, Rosemary West's belly began to swell with her third child. Heather (Rose and Fred's first biological daughter) was two and a half, baby Mae June was just ten months old and Rose's stepdaughter Anne Marie was eight. There should have been a fourth place at the table, but Rosemary had already murdered little Charmaine, who was eight years old when she died.

And Rosemary herself was not yet 21.

Other youngsters her age in Britain were leading a very different life from her. The early seventies were birthing a new era of counterculture, with young people searching for identity and fanning the flames of rebellion in clothing, music and drug experimentation. Alternative music created by the likes of David Bowie and Pink Floyd was taking the country by storm, and while some joined the burgeoning punk movement that was rising up, others embraced the new and increasingly mainstream aesthetic of 'peasant shirts', leather jackets, platform shoes and bell bottoms.

The post-war economic boom that had fuelled the economy was tailing off, oil prices were up and industrial strikes were on the rise, while civil rights movements were gathering momentum, as was the struggle for women's liberation.

Against this backdrop of upheaval, Rose's life stood in sharp contrast. The domestic realm was her domain, a realm that outwardly seemed composed of meals, nappies, and laundry round the clock while she nurtured her young family.

In reality, though, that realm was already marked by her tempestuous screaming at the children, her sex-for-money escapades in an upstairs room with a custom-made peephole through which Fred could enjoy the visual spectacle, and a mind that enjoyed reliving the twisted pleasures she had indulged in on the night Caroline Owens was kidnapped and dragged to 25 Cromwell Street.

The unborn child in Rosemary's belly at that time was a little boy – her first son – who would be called Stephen when he was born in 1973. By then, Fred West was 33 and liked to keep himself busy. Ever the handyman around the house, he had converted more of the rooms in the family home into bedsits for lodgers while also holding down his day job in the local area as a builder. He was also already a hardened killer. By then, Fred had murdered his girlfriend Anne McFall, dismembered and buried his stepdaughter Charmaine, murdered, dismembered and buried his wife Rena, and abducted, tortured and raped Caroline Owens.

Generally speaking, they still appeared to be an unremarkable average couple living in small-town England with no trace to the outside world of their already sinister and twisted past.

It would be remiss here not to mention another young woman who went missing five years prior and who had been featured in all the local papers as her family desperately searched for her.

Mary Bastholm, born the year before Rosemary West in 1952, was only fifteen years old and a waitress at the Pop-In, a small and basic cafe that sat less than a mile from 25 Cromwell Street and at which Fred West, who would only meet Rosemary at a bus stop the following year, was a regular customer.

On 6 January 1968, she sat at a bus stop in Bristol Road, Gloucester, in freezing cold weather waiting for a bus so she could go and visit her boyfriend, Tim Merrett. Slung over the shoulder of her blue outfit was a bag containing a Monopoly set that belonged to Tim but had been at Mary's house since their last game. Their plan was to have a cosy night in, playing board games and hunkering down from the cold weather outside. Tim, a biker who also frequented the cafe where Mary worked, along with many other motorbike enthusiasts, would have gone to Mary's house that cold night but his bike was out of commission, and so he was stuck at home fixing it when they made their plans for the night ahead.

That same night, it began to snow so heavily that buses were eventually taken off the road, and it is not known if Mary actually made it onto a bus before the service was cancelled or if she was offered a lift by a regular customer she knew from the cafe.

But either way, she never made it to Tim's house. He called her parents to find out where she was after she didn't arrive. Her parents and two older brothers, Peter and Martin, began to worry but expected that a few minutes later they would locate her.

The first place her mother checked was the house across the road where Mary's best friend Christine Ford lived. If Mary was anywhere but with her boyfriend, she could well be at Christine's house, her mother reasoned.

The two girls had lived in their respective houses since birth and had been inseparable. Chris, as Mary called her, found her friend to be rather headstrong on occasion, but mainly a quiet and gentle soul. The two girls had always done everything together – walking to and from school, buying little cupcakes en route, playing hopscotch in the road, catching tadpoles in the reservoir, and later, giggling at the regular Friday night disco as the local boys, whom they had ignored for years, became of interest to them. They even looked after their pet tortoises together, with Chris doing her best to comfort Mary when she was inconsolable after hers died.

The two, like many young girls, used to spend hours in one another's bedrooms chatting, gossiping and sharing seemingly insignificant details of their day with one another. Mary had mentioned to Chris that there was a regular customer at the cafe named Fred West and that he often did construction in the area and was going to do some work on the cafe itself. But she said nothing else about him and the conversation switched to other topics.

On the night Mary was supposed to turn up at Tim's house but didn't, Tim called her parents to find out where she was, and that was when panic set in. Imagining she might have been in an accident, her desperate parents and boyfriend swung into action, first calling the local hospitals to see if anyone fitting her description had been brought in. No, they were told.

From a loving home and with no history of rebelling against her family, Mary was not earmarked as someone at all likely to run away. It would have been highly out of character, and her family was now convinced something terrible had happened. They quickly alerted the police, and shortly thereafter, a massive manhunt of around three hundred searchers was mounted. Helicopters were sent to survey from the skies, and trackers were deployed on the ground.

All they found in the snow were pieces of the monopoly set, but no sign of Mary or her clothing.

The search continued, with a photograph of Mary doing the rounds in the community.

In that photograph, she is in a formal pale dress with her hair piled into a neat version of a beehive on top of her head with a large flower attached. She is wearing long gloves and gives a soft smile for the camera, her crescent-shaped eyes twinkling.

It is one of the last pictures ever taken of Mary Bastholm, and one that her parents clung to for comfort in the years that followed as they tried to come to terms with her sudden disappearance.

***

Fast forward to early spring 1973, by which time the Bastholm family had all but given up on ever finding their beloved daughter who had gone missing five years prior. Four months had passed since Rosemary and Fred had received nothing more than a slap on the wrist from the legal system for abducting and assaulting Caroline Owens. Fred had seen the night with Caroline as a 'test for Rose' to see if she approved of his 'sex life', and she had clearly passed with flying colours.

But it had been a close call for Rosemary and Fred. It was the first time they had carried out their twisted sexual torture together on another person, and though their punishment was meagre, they had been reported and caught.

Clearly, however, they had not been deterred.

One day a new lodger arrived at the door. Eighteen years old and with his best friend Alan Davies at his side, Benjamin Stanniland was the picture of youth. Carrying their bags off to their new room, the two boys felt confident this was the perfect place to lodge for this time in their lives.

Then, on their very first night there, something strange happened.

Rose West, the woman of the house, slipped into their room and lay down between the two men on a bed where they were chatting. She said she wanted to have sex with them, and the boys were rather pleased at the offer.

It only happened that one time, but at the very least it gave the boys a glimpse into the type of household they had entered, a house where an obsession with sex was the norm, at least for the couple that owned the abode.

Shortly after that, Benjamin's eyes landed on a beautiful girl at a cafe. Her name was Lynda Gough, and she had silky auburn shoulder-length hair and wore stylish horn-rimmed glasses that pointed up at the ends, as was the fashion of the day.

Soon after that first meeting, Lynda agreed to go out on a date with Benjamin, and their romance flourished in the days and weeks that followed.

Nineteen years old and from a protective family, Lynda was starting to spread her wings. She had lived in Gloucester all her life and had just finished her studies at a private school in Midland Road. Now, on the brink of adulthood and in the first flush of her romance with Benjamin, she would often head off to 25 Cromwell Street to visit him.

Rose and Fred took note of the frequent visitor and soon struck up a friendship with her. They went on to ask her to do some shifts as a nanny to their children. Although she still loved her parents very much, she was getting a taste of freedom and was going through what her mother called 'a minor teenage rebellion'. When they offered her a place to stay, she accepted.

Her father John was a fireman and her mother June a clerical worker. They were well-meaning citizens and had raised Lynda with a deep sense of principles and being community-minded. Her school life had been a cosseted experience, and she had gone on to become a rather talented seamstress, proudly getting her first job at a co-op in Brunswick Road.

Though her parents were sad to see her leave the family home, they understood her need for independence when she left a note in April 1973 for them that read: 'Please don't worry about me. I have got a flat and I will come and see you sometime. Love, Lyn.'

By then, Lynda and Benjamin had gone their separate ways and Lynda was starting her 'new life' at the lodgings at 25 Cromwell Street. Her parents expected her to still pop in, phone them and come over for a meal, but ten days passed since they'd read her note and there was no word at all from their loving daughter.

Now the dread began to set in. They informed a local police officer who was also a family friend that they had not heard from Lynda, but they understood that she was not yet considered an at-risk person.

June now contacted some of Lynda's friends and explained that she wanted to check up on Lynda as she'd become worried. They told her that Lynda was staying with homeowners at 25 Cromwell Street, and June was relieved to finally have an address, so she set off in search of her daughter, who was one of three Gough children.

June walked up to the front door of the dreary three-storey house at the end of a row of semis and knocked. A woman with a fleshy face, dark hair and big glasses opened it and introduced herself as Rose.

Now two strange things happened that might have turned June cold had she not been staring into the eyes of a psychopath who was able to lie with a deadpan face.

Firstly, June had an eerie sense she had met the woman before. As the pieces fell into place, she seemed to recall meeting Rose – or a woman who looked very much like her – a month prior, when she had come to the door of the family home asking after Lynda. She thought she must be mistaken, however, when Rose denied that Lynda was living there and took it even further, claiming she had never even met Lynda before.

But then June looked down, and the second and far more disturbing piece of the puzzle fell into place, giving her a shock as she stood there: Rose was wearing a pair of slippers that she instantly recognised as belonging to her daughter, as well as a cardigan that too belonged to Lynda. Looking around, she also noticed some of her daughter's clothes on a washing line.

June said this to Rose, who now, cool as a cucumber, changed her story without blinking. She made it seem like her memory had been jogged and that she did, after all, remember Lynda. She now told June that, in fact, Lynda had stayed there for a very short time a while ago but had since moved on. Fred now also appeared in the doorway but stood beside Rose and said nothing.

Rosemary told the anxious mother that her daughter had left for Weston-super-Mare, a seaside resort an hour south down the M5, and that she had left her slippers and clothes behind on her departure.

She also went the route of feigning compassion for June and simulating a mother-to-mother moment of understanding how much love and anxiety goes into raising children. She told June that it was sad how children sometimes had no respect for their parents or understanding of their feelings, and seldom showed any gratitude for the opportunities they had been given.

June Gough left the house still anxious yet convinced her daughter was not at 25 Cromwell Street. She reported her missing to the police a few days later, approached the Salvation Army, and also travelled to Weston-super-Mare in search of her daughter.

But nothing turned up.

Like Mary Bastholm's family, the Goughs must have stared into their beautiful young daughter's face in a photograph for years after, wondering where on Earth she could be. In the case of the Goughs, it is a poignant photo of Lynda standing near the fireplace at the family home. She is wearing a cowl-necked sky-blue dress with thin amber and white stripes running up and down and across. With a broad and beaming smile and her hair held back in an Alice band typical of the time, she is the picture of youth, and no doubt, that self-same picture must have haunted her parents and two siblings for decades after she went missing.

Any news or closure they so desperately sought at the time would only come two decades later.

***

On 10 April 1958, a little girl named Carole Ann Cooper was born in Luton, Bedfordshire. The town, quickly gaining popularity for its airport built in the late 1930s just an hour from London, was also prospering thanks to a motor industry boom. The Coopers were one of many families who had moved into the area as housing estates popped up and the density of the population grew virtually overnight.

At this particular time, Rosemary West was only four years old and living some 250 miles away in Devon under the watchful eye of her obsessive-compulsive father and depressed mother. Not much is known about Carole's early childhood but one can safely assume her mother held her in her arms that day at the hospital after she had just entered the world.

This mother-daughter bond would not be given time to develop, however. When Carole was still a very small girl, her mother passed away and the fate of her life took an unwelcome turn. She was left in the care of her father Colin at a time when men were notoriously spared the daily challenges of meeting the never-ending needs of little ones.

It did not take long, however, before another woman entered Carole's life. Her father remarried, and far from taking the place of nurturing care her biological mum might have provided, Carole's stepmother was not very interested in raising her. She wanted a child of her own, and soon, little Nigel, her half-brother, entered the world.

But, as it turns out, Carole's father eventually found that his second wife was not quite the lifelong romantic partner he had hoped for. Just a few years after tying the knot, the two found themselves at the divorce court. Nigel, then two, naturally remained with his mother, but Carole's fate hung in the balance.

Without looking back, her father simply packed his bags and left the area for good. Carole was only fifteen at the time, and she was enrolled at the Christopher Whitehead Girls School in Worcester.

Carole was the picture of youthful beauty. She had neat lips, clear blue eyes and wavy hair that just touched the shoulder of her school blouse. Like the other girls at the school, every morning she would put on the blouse, along with the thick skirt and striped tie that formed the uniform of the school. But, under the one sleeve, she hid a tattoo that the teachers didn't know about. Nothing could be more poignant than how she now had to make sense of her world: while many tattoo the names of lovers, children or lost ones on their bodies, Carole had her own nickname, Caz, tattooed on her left forearm. She was, after all, without her mother and father, and she was destined to now fend for herself.

It is not known how she ended up there, but Carole arrived at the tall wooden fence of the The Pines children's home in Bilford Road, Worcester, one of many council facilities for children in the area. The home had a humble sign outside with white lettering, and the inside, not unexpectedly, was designed for quantity over quality: there were many children needing a bed, a few square meals a day, and adults to watch over them in the absence of their own parents.

The young residents would need to seek permission if they were to spend the night anywhere else, and Carole duly notified the staff on Saturday 10 November 1973 that she wished to sleep over at the home of the only family member who still cared about her: her grandmother who lived in Warndon just three miles away. Carole, or perhaps her grandmother, had chosen The Pines because it meant such visits would be easy and Carole would be spared the hassle and dangers of travelling long distances.

The plan was set. She would get together with her boyfriend and head down to the local cinema. After watching the movie, she would enjoy the freedom of the city for a few hours and then hop on a bus and get out at the nearest stop by her grandmother's house.

And for the most part, all went according to plan.

It was late afternoon and, bundled warmly in her jacket against the biting November air, she met her boyfriend on the small concrete steps outside the Odeon Cinema just below the bridge that crosses over the busy section of Foregate Street. They held hands, ate popcorn and giggled with their friends. After that, they hopped on a bus and headed off to a pub on Brickfields Road.

Just after 9 p.m., Carole waved her boyfriend goodbye and made her way to the closest bus stop so she could get to her grandmother's house in Warndon. Her grandmother, for her part, awaited the teenage girl's arrival, happy that she'd had an evening out with her boyfriend and maybe some friends but looking forward to spending time with her.

She waited for Carole, looking out of the window now and then and expecting to see her silhouetted against the lights in the street.

But this never happened.

Carole Ann did not arrive, and at some point, her grandmother began to panic.

She headed down to the police station, where she reported that the girl was missing, but no manhunt was ever launched. The reasons for this are not clear, but according to the records, children living in institutional care were often assumed to have simply run away when they went missing. Added to this was the lack of any evidence suggesting foul play, but most importantly, Carole was not of much interest to the authorities because she was not from the right 'class' in a very socially stratified England. Had she been from a more prominent family, the police might have been helpful in trying to locate her.

But instead, like Lynda Gough, she seemingly vanished into thin air and was never seen alive again.

***

It was only in January the following year that the police began to join dots that could link Carole's disappearance to that of another young girl — though six years older than Carole — from a more socially prominent family. One would imagine that the assault on Caroline Owens, followed by the cold case of Lynda Gough less than a year before Carole Ann Cooper disappeared, might have aroused some suspicion among police of a modus operandi by a single killer or killers. Even the case of Mary Bastholm, six years prior, might have been linked had the police been more astute and the technology of record-keeping a little more sophisticated.

But it took the case of Lucy Partington to rouse the authorities into action.

Lucy was born on 4 March 1952 in St Albans, a town north of London often described as 'posh' in the class-obsessed society of the United Kingdom. Her early years were spent in this commuter town twenty miles north of the capital city before she later moved with her family to the Gloucestershire village of Gretton in the Cotswolds, where they lived in a converted cider mill.

Lucy was adored by her parents, Roger (a chemist) and Margaret (an architect), her older siblings, Marian and David, and her younger brother, Mark, in their well-to-do but bohemian academic household. Lucy was very close to her siblings, especially her sister Marian. Later, when Lucy was still small, her parents would split and her mother would remarry Martin Bernal, a literary scholar, when Lucy was eight years old.

Her extended family represented some of the icons of British literature. Her uncle was Kingsley Amis, knighted as a 'sir' for his extraordinary achievements, which included the publication of over twenty novels and several poetry and short story collections. He was also a high achiever in the world of academia, and his young niece Lucy had shown ambitions to follow a similar path.

Lucy's cousin Martin Amis was three years her senior, and he too went on to become a literary genius with cult-like status in the world of books, winning several awards and earning a reputation as one of the most original voices in modern British literature.

It is because of this wordsmith cousin of hers that Lucy, as a child, is forever memorialised in her uniqueness, unlike many of the other victims, whose poorer socio-economic status meant no such tributes would ever be forthcoming.

Writing in the *Guardian* newspaper, Martin Amis described his cousin Lucy when she was a child as follows:

> When I go back to the core of my childhood, my cousin Lucy seems always to be in the peripheral vision of my memories. She is off to one side, always off to one side, with a book, with a scheme or a project or an enterprise.

Or with an animal. I keep thinking that if I could only shift my head an inch and change its angle, then I would see her fully. Just as Marian, her sister, a year my senior, was magnified in my mind, so Lucy, two and a half years younger, was additionally reduced. Only their brother David did I see four-square ... In my clearest image of her she is crossing the small courtyard between the stable and the house, looking downwards and smiling secretively, privately, as if sharing a joke with the mouse I knew she had in her pocket. Some people, alas, live and die without trace. They come and they go and they leave no trace. This, at least, was not Lucy's destiny.

She was destined for great things. She was studying English literature at the esteemed Exeter University and had grown up in a stable environment under the loving eye of her parents and siblings.

By November of 1973, at the age of 21, Lucy and her inquiring mind had discovered religious scriptures as texts to be scrutinised with the same rigour as any academic text. This focus, according to the records, had led her down the path to Catholicism and the chaste lifestyle that came with it, and she was determined to focus very hard on her final year studies, which she hoped to complete after the Christmas break.

With her wavy auburn hair, funky glasses, polo necks and flared pants, Lucy was the picture of left-wing student politics of the time. The only thing she had in common with Rosemary West at this point was her age. While Lucy was gentle, serious and bookish, Rosemary was violent, poorly educated and unpredictable. She was already a mother and, unbeknownst to the world, a murderer.

In December of 1973, a month after committing herself to Catholicism, Lucy made the two-hundred-mile trip home from

Exeter to Gretton to celebrate Christmas with her family in the Cotswolds. Like so many other families across the country, they caught up with their news, opened gifts, ate home-cooked food, and kept warm in front of the fire in the thick of winter on Christmas Day. Lucy was particularly delighted to receive a Victorian jar from Marian, her beloved sister.

Boxing Day was spent in the company of family, and on the day after that, Lucy had planned to head out to the upmarket Pittville area of Cheltenham, well known for its natural spas, manicured parks and beautiful Georgian architecture. Lucy had planned to visit her friend Helen Render, who lived in an upmarket house there, a hundred miles away from Lucy's own home. Her brother David gave her a lift and offered to fetch her later on her return, but she declined and insisted that she wanted to catch the bus instead.

He would later say that in the car on the drive there, they chatted about his new girlfriend, whom he knew was not the type of woman Lucy could relate to, a woman he jokingly described in his own words as 'sexy but thick'. He felt he had to justify their relationship to his bright younger sister, but that she, in turn, was not critical at all and he felt no sense of judgement from her.

Lucy was excited to see Helen. They were both passionate about the world of academia and were old friends. They spent the evening discussing what the future might hold. The two had formed a bond in the world of academia, so much so that on the day of that visit, they spent hours working on Lucy's application for postgraduate studies in medieval art at the Courtauld Institute of Art in London.

The hours had flown by and soon enough, it was after ten in the evening. Lucy hugged her friend goodbye and started the three-minute walk from her friend's affluent house to the nearest bus station. In her bag was the Courtauld application, the beautiful jar from her sister, and a letter she was planning to post.

She also carried with her a book, a fourteenth century mediaeval poem entitled 'Pearl'.

Lucy made her way to the Pittville Pump Room bus stop on Evesham Road. This section of the main arterial road was the kind of area in which nobody imagined any danger could lurk. She crossed a few roads and hurried to catch the 10.30 p.m. bus that went via Bishops Cleeve and would end up near her family home in Gretton.

As it happened, there was a strike on the go in the country at the time, and the street lighting was off. This meant the bus stop was not bathed in its usual pool of light. As a result, nobody would ever come forward to offer testimony about seeing Lucy either en route to or waiting at the bus stop. But what was clear was that she never posted her letter, despite the fact that there was a postbox en route, and that she never made it onto the bus.

Piecing it together, it is very likely the Wests came driving past in their grey car, most likely on the prowl rather than simply driving past by coincidence, and either offered the 21-year-old a lift or bundled her into the car against her will. She was not a frequent hitchhiker and had made it clear that she had every intention of catching the 10.30 bus. Perhaps she saw the bus pulling away up ahead, and perhaps Rosemary's presence reassured the unsuspecting Lucy that this was just a warm and friendly couple, maybe even a family if baby Stephen was with them, and that there was nothing to fear.

Given that it was cold and dark, hopping in their car likely seemed a better option than waiting for a bus to arrive, and off they went.

Meanwhile, back at Lucy's family home in Gretton, nobody had any idea she was not en route home. The family members all headed off to bed, assured that Lucy would catch the bus – as she had insisted to her brother David, who had offered a lift – arrive home, and simply let herself in and climb into bed.

The following morning, her mother Margaret went into the room to wake her up but, to her horror, found the room empty and the bed still made. Blind terror set in as she knew the plan was very clear: Lucy would catch the bus home from Helen and they'd eat breakfast together the following morning.

Margaret now hurried to the police station to notify the police.

But she soon faced the same blank stares that Lynda Gough's family had faced. The police did not take it too seriously at first, implying, as they did, that young people often weren't where they said they would be for various reasons.

But, when a police officer arrived at the family home in Gretton, knocked on the door and began questioning the Partingtons about Lucy and her possible whereabouts, he quickly realised she was far from being the type of youngster who would simply get up and go out without informing anyone of her whereabouts.

Unlike for many of the previous victims whose disappearance either sparked no major concern among any family members or did not stir the police to action, in the case of Lucy Partington, an extensive manhunt was set in motion.

As a first step, the local police undertook to carry out widespread searches. Next, they made inquiries around Helen's neighbourhood, trying to trace Lucy's steps in the area where she had last been seen. The family, for their part, also worked tirelessly to find her. Missing posters popped up around the city that read: 'This girl has been missing since 10.15 pm Thursday, 27th Dec. 1973. Was last seen in Albemarle Gate, Pittville, Cheltenham. 21 yrs. 5′4″long dark curly hair, gold rimmed specs, dressed in rust coloured raincoat, pink jeans, red mittens. Carrying faded brown canvas satchel.'

The case received significant media attention, with newspaper articles and broadcasts aimed at raising public awareness about her disappearance. The police also drew a dotted line between the mystery of her disappearance and that of Carole Ann, who had vanished one and a half months earlier.

But, as the hours turned to days and the days to weeks and then months and years, the desperation – peppered sometimes with hope – of the Partington family turned into grief without closure, an open-ended agony that could not heal.

For Lucy's brother, David, the mystery was untenable. He coped by convincing himself that Lucy was definitely alive but had chosen to live elsewhere. The family imagined an endless parade of scenarios of the life that Lucy might be living, even feeling angry towards her for absconding.

But in the backs of their minds, all must have suspected full well that Lucy was the last person on Earth who would wilfully run away from her family and never make contact.

To admit that, however, would be to admit their deepest fear of all.

***

By the spring of 1974, when the Partingtons were facing the horror of Lucy's disappearance becoming yet another cold case, the Wests had proven to each other that they were willing to harm and kill any girls and young women in their orbit. Their victims by then fell into three categories, each one representing a concentric circle either closer to or further away from the sexually twisted and bloodthirsty couple.

Those nearest to them were the ones knitted into their domestic fabric – Anne McFall, who had been Fred's lover; little Charmaine, who was his stepdaughter; and Rena, who was his ex-lover and Charmaine's mother.

Then there were the women who were caught in the spider web that the couple had spun by using their home as a place of lodging, or by luring young women to work as nannies at that same household with free accommodation thrown into the mix. Caroline Owens, the only escapee, had been the first in this category. Then came Lynda Gough, who by April 1974 had been missing for exactly a year, with her desperate family still searching to no avail.

And then there were victims who were increasingly becoming the Wests' most common targets: unsuspecting strangers in need of transport who were tricked into accepting a lift from a seemingly pleasant husband and wife and their small children. Carole Ann Cooper and Lucy Partington had both been abducted at a bus stop, and very likely, Mary Bastholm too.

The next two victims of Fred and Rosemary West would also fall into this third category. They were both young women with their adult lives stretched out before them, and they were both the hapless victims of a terrible fate: being in the wrong place at the wrong time and thus falling into the hands of the Wests with their unquenchable libidos and bloodlust.

The first of these two was Therese Siegenthaler.

Like Lucy, she was born the year before Rosemary, and it is strange to think that under very different circumstances, both Lucy and Therese might have met Rosemary as a peer with the same path laid out: the fun of being young and carefree, studying to further oneself, and maybe dreaming of marriage and childbearing as something for later in life.

Therese was born on 27 November 1952 at Trub in Switzerland, a place of sparsely populated villages dotted along rolling green hills and woodlands. Her family moved to the beautiful city of Bern, which, like many other first-world cities during the fifties, represented a prosperous life made easier by the rise of new commodities and consumption. Therese spent a happy childhood there and, at the age of sixteen, left school to enrol in a diploma course in secretarial studies.

At the age of twenty, after working for a few years in her home country, she packed her bags and headed off on an adventure to the United Kingdom, where she wanted to take her studies further and get some exciting travel done.

In early 1973, Therese arrived in the capital and found her way to the south-east region of the city where she filled in the various forms to enrol at the Woolwich College of Further Education. She enrolled in a sociology course and was excited when she found accommodation six miles away in Caterham Road, Lewisham, a five-minute walk from the vibrant high street. The area by then had become a commercial and transport hub, and Therese was likely in awe of the magnitude of a city like London, which, in comparison, would have made Bern seem tiny.

Therese settled into the rhythm of her new life far from home, and she soon found the ideal weekend job to earn money for living expenses and saving up for travel. Just five years before, the Swiss Centre opened its doors in Leicester Square. It was established as a showcase for Swiss culture in the heart of London since the Swiss community around that area had grown in both stature and size over more than a century.

Therese was the ideal candidate for a casual job there, adding an air of authenticity to an establishment that included a Swiss bank and several Swiss-themed restaurants and souvenir shops. It also placed her in the heart of the city, where she could experience the excitement of being there on the brink of her adult years while also squirrelling away some money for exploring other parts of the UK.

By April 1974, she had been in London for more than a year and was fully immersed in her studies and weekend job. But, with the Easter holidays and a break from lectures looming, she booked herself a ticket to travel via Holyhead to Ireland, where she had planned to visit a friend in Dublin on her arrival.

On 15 April, the petite Therese dressed for the day ahead: a warm pair of trousers and a black mid-length PVC jacket, typical of the era, with a belt around the waist. With her family far away in Switzerland, it was left to the friends she'd made in the UK to see her off on her adventure.

Edith Simmons, her closest friend, caught wind of Therese's plan to hitch from London to the ferry port at Holyhead three hundred miles away. While today that might be frowned upon, in the 1970s hitching was a very common way for both men and women to get around the country, and Therese thought nothing of it. Edith, however, had major doubts. She had a bad feeling about the potential dangers of the plan and begged her friend to catch the train instead. But the hard-working Therese said she did not want to spend the cash she had earned at the Swiss Centre on a train ticket and would stick with her plan. Now feeling even more worried, Edith pressed the money for a train ticket into Therese's hand and made her promise she would not get into any stranger's car. And the two friends went their separate ways.

Therese was touched that her friend cared so much, and according to some reports, she did first board a train but then later changed her mind and reverted to her original plan.

Had she not done so, she might still be alive today and might have spent her adult years, as her friend later reflected, as a 'brilliant advocate for human rights,' or 'a diplomat'.

It never came to light where it happened, but at some point, Therese had the same fateful moment as others before her: as she stood on the side of the road, watching the cars passing by through the lenses of her thick-rimmed glasses, a grey car pulled up, and there smiling back at her was the gap-toothed grin of Fred West, likely with Rose and one or more of the children in tow, creating the picture of a 'normal' and harmless family.

Therese never made it to Holyhead to catch the ferry.

This in itself did not raise any suspicion – many young travellers change their plans, go with the flow, meet other travellers who invite them to join in for an adventure in another direction. And, without the technology we have today, there was nothing strange about her not having made contact with family or friends for a few days. It was simply assumed that she was in Dublin with her friend, having a great time and much-needed holiday fun during her Easter break.

But then the holidays ended and still there was no sign of Therese, not at her accommodation or when her college opened its doors again for the new term. Eleven days had now passed since she was last seen, and she was long since due back.

On 26 April, her disappearance was reported at Lee Road Police Station.

The metropolitan police swung into action, and her family was notified in Switzerland that she had gone missing.

Just as it was for the other families before them, shock, hope and horror came and went in waves for the Siegenthalers, but Therese Siegenthaler had seemingly vanished into thin air.

Unlike Lucy's family, who tried to process their grief by writing books about her and sharing their tragedy with the outside world, the Siegenthalers tried to process theirs by staying firmly outside of the public gaze. Theirs was a journey of heartache that unfolded behind the closed doors of their house in Bern, and like the others, two decades would pass before the horrible truth would reveal itself.

***

THREE YOUNG WOMEN, NO POLICE SUSPICION

On 26 June 1959, a warm summer's day in Birmingham in the Midlands of England, little Shirley Lloyd came into the world, but the map laid out for her short life would not be an easy one.

When Shirley was just two years of age, her parents split up and she was put into care.

By that time, Rosemary West was herself just a child of eight, and another thirteen years would pass before Shirley would be lured into the dark and depraved world of 25 Cromwell Street.

The fact that Shirley Lloyd was also known as Shirley Owen and later as Shirley Hubbard bears testimony to the fact that her identity in this world was never clearly inscribed on anyone's family tree ... though she longed for that kind of security and belonging.

It was in 1972, the year she became a teenager, that Shirley decided to change her surname to Hubbard. She had been fostered by a family with that surname since the age of six, and, although the name change never became official, it provides a glimpse into Shirley's desire to feel like she belonged somewhere, to feel like a 'normal' teenage girl living with her own family.

Her foster father, Jim Hubbard, was a social worker for Worcestershire social services, and perhaps that was how he came upon her. According to the records, Shirley was 'pretty, spirited and vulnerable', and it's likely that these were the traits that convinced Jim Hubbard that he and his family could turn her life around so that she harnessed her spiritedness in the right direction.

Shirley spent her early teenage years living in Ombersley Road in the canal-side town of Droitwich with the Hubbards. The town, twenty miles from her birthplace of Birmingham, was increasingly connected to surrounding metropolitan areas around the time of Shirley's childhood as transport hubs, especially bus routes, grew thick and fast in all directions.

New housing estates were also popping up overnight, and perhaps Shirley, like other teenage girls of the era, imagined one day she would be married, have children of her own – whom she would never give up to the system – and would buy a house in the area so she could build as normal a life as possible. She also had ambitions to learn whatever she could and become a successful breadwinner when she was older.

In November of 1974, when she was fifteen years old and preparing to finish her education at Droitwich High School the following year, she enrolled in a pre-leaving school course that included some hands-on work experience. To this end, she was doing the seven-mile commute in and out of Worcester, where she was assigned shifts at the Debenhams department store at the Crowngate Shopping Centre as part of the course. On 14 November 1974, with the winter sun setting early and Shirley having been on her feet in the store all day, the teenager stepped outside into the cold street. She met her boyfriend and the two wandered around a fair in the area, eating fish and chips while she unwound after a busy day.

She was then ready to catch one of the buses that shuttled people out of the city centre to surrounding towns like Droitwich.

If this day had unfolded like the ones before it, she would have sat at the bus stop, patiently waiting. She would have boarded the first bus to come along and done the seven-mile ride home with streets turning dark outside. Perhaps she would have stared out of the bus window, with the nighttime only spurring her dreams for a cosy domestic life like the one the Hubbards had shown her.

But she never did make it onto the bus; or, if she did, she never made it home.

When it became clear that Shirley had disappeared, it was reported to the police, but as was (and still often is) the case with any child who has been in state care or foster homes, the police did not register it as a serious situation; they assumed she was a runaway, and they did not wish to spend major resources on looking for her. That said, some attempts at least were made, but nothing turned up.

And that was how Shirley Hubbard, a girl who was only fifteen and was the same age when she disappeared as Rosemary West was when she met Fred, joined the dreaded catalogue of missing young women whose names would only be linked together two decades later when the police finally made their grim excavations at Cromwell Street.

***

By 1975, it seems that Rosemary West and her depraved and much older husband Fred had figured out the 'perfect' formula for their chain of miserable murders. By then, at least four young women or girls had had the sheer misfortune of ending up in the Wests' torturous hands, and their modus operandi of procuring their victims had clearly switched from preying on those in their social circle or family to those trying to hitch a ride or catch a bus.

And it is a sad fact that the names of these young women and girls will forever be etched in history as the victims of Rosemary and Fred West when, in fact, they all had their lives ahead of them like any other youngster – dreaming of a future, having fun, and just being out in the world. We would not even know their names or be writing or reading about them had they not met this terrible fate.

And so it was for Juanita Mott, yet another child of only fifteen who was in the wrong place at the wrong time, with disastrous consequences.

Juanita was born on 1 February 1957, less than four years after Rosemary West. She was an outgoing person who loved to connect with others, not least her two older sisters, Belinda and Mary-Ann. Their mother had been abandoned as a child and, in her adult life, had suffered from severe depression. This could not have been easy on the three girls, seeing their single mother struggle through each day as she tried to raise them as best she could on a shoestring budget after their dad absconded when Juanita was still little.

They were intermittently put into care and taken out again, not because their mother didn't want them but because she couldn't manage. Her love for them was never in doubt, though, and she always seemed to get them back.

At the age of fifteen, Juanita moved out of the family home. She was quite rebellious by then and loved going out to parties and staying over at friends. She did not lose her connection with the family, however, and would often sneak in through the window for a quick warm bath and a change of clothing.

Had things gone differently, these might have just been funny stories shared at Juanita's later birthdays, or at her wedding, perhaps, but in light of what was to follow, her being a bit of a party animal would come to bear on the way her disappearance was perceived.

Strangely enough, according to the records, Juanita at some point had a boyfriend who had befriended Fred West during one of his short stints in prison for theft. This would later raise the question of whether Juanita had actually rented space at 25 Cromwell Street at some point, having caught wind of affordable lodgings on offer there.

This would never be proven either way, with the other more plausible theory being that it was merely a coincidence and that Juanita had met the Wests as a chance encounter.

THREE YOUNG WOMEN, NO POLICE SUSPICION

In April 1975, five months after young Shirley Hubbard had seemingly vanished into thin air, Juanita was due to help out some friends who were getting married. Juanita was living a life of so-called 'sofa surfing' at the time, moving from one friend's house to another with nothing but a bag of clothes in her possession. This could not have been an easy life for a teenager, and surely her mother and sisters must have worried on more than one occasion about whether this lifestyle was safe for the beautiful Juanita with her deep brown eyes and sculpted face. But by the time she turned eighteen in February 1975, they likely felt more confident that she could take care of herself. Add to this the fact that this area of Gloucestershire is dotted with small towns where everybody knows everybody's business, and Newent, where she happened to be staying at the time, was no exception. Her mother and sisters were also in Newent – some ten miles from Gloucester – and always had at least a vague sense of her whereabouts.

On Saturday 12 April 1975, Juanita's friend was excited for her wedding day. What could be better than a spring wedding in this beautiful part of the country? Juanita had offered to babysit her friend's children so that she could have a carefree day and focus on the wedding.

But as time ticked by, Juanita did not arrive for her babysitting duties. Her not showing up for babysitting likely raised the ire of those around her. Sure, she loved partying and was prone to running off for days on end, but this was a promise she had made to her friend and she was now letting everyone down.

When the wedding was about to begin, Juanita had still not shown up, and so the bride-to-be had to scramble, and she called up one of Juanita's sisters to do the babysitting instead. All the while, it must have seemed that Juanita was doing what Juanita always did: going with the flow instead of taking life seriously.

But then the wedding ended and there was still no sign. The next day was the same and the day after that. Days turned into weeks, and Juanita was gone. But still, the family believed that the rebellious Juanita must have run off to begin a new life elsewhere.

It was only years later that Belinda Mott, who had been heartbroken believing her sister had run away and cut contact, now considered the possibility of a much more worrying reality.

And so she began a serious search for her sister, at a time when there was no internet, no social media, no digital record of who had been where at what time. It was an upward slog that literally meant going through phone books, checking in at benefits centres to see if she had ever come in to sign on and collect the dole, and searching hospital records and any other database that existed in a pre-digital world.

But it was all to no avail. Juanita was well and truly gone from sight. Appeals to the media also brought nothing, and just like the other families before them, the Motts were now immersed in a world of intermittent hope, heartache and utter frustration.

In a disturbing twist of fate, during the years that Belinda searched for her sister, she would sometimes visit a friend who had moved into a casual boarding house.

The address was 25 Cromwell Street.

7

Rosemary's Stepchild

While the police never seemed to join the dots of all the girls who had gone missing in the area during the 1970s, there was certainly one set of eyes that had seen far more than they should have. Or little ears that maybe heard the screams coming from somewhere down below in her family home. That child was Anne Marie West, the subdued little girl whose sense of 'normal life' was warped by the time she was old enough to have any inkling of the world around her.

She was eight years old when she stepped through the doors of the new family home in Cromwell Street and put her bags in the room where she was told she would be sleeping. By then, it's important to remember, she had already experienced extreme abuse and violence, both physical and psychological in nature. Already etched on her memory was the image of her mother Rena being beaten up and screamed at by her father Fred, or the many times she was spirited off to someone else's caravan by Anne McFall and Isa McNeill in an attempt to shield her from her father's rage, before those two women disappeared from her life.

Her life had already been filled with challenges that most regular children could not have dreamed about: the trauma of seeing her mother drive away from the caravan with Isa, the only two women who ever really loved her; the agony of seeing her sister punished over and over again by Rose and then disappearing so suddenly; the confusion of believing that her sister could return to Scotland while she could not. Amidst the pain, there must have been a dose of jealousy and anger. Why would they just leave her there with these monsters? What had she done to deserve this?

And so, when she settled into her room at 25 Cromwell Street, it was without her sister Charmaine who had always been both her companion and her feisty protector, who stood up to the adults when Anne Marie herself preferred to sink into the shadows.

Life in the new family home was bewildering and frightening. A petite girl with the same crescent-shaped eyes as her mother, Anne Marie watched her father setting to work converting the second floor into rooms for rent and a 'workplace' for Rose. She would have learned very quickly to recognise the sound of the doorbell that only her mother would answer. The red light outside 'Mandy's' room meant she should stay out, and this was just one of a myriad things that the little girl had to frame in her mind as being 'normal' when in fact it was the complete opposite.

It was at the age of eight, once they had brought their belongings to their new home and settled in, that a life already marked by severe trauma and loss was about to get a whole lot worse.

This new magnitude of horror began one day when she was alone at home with her father and stepmother, and she was dragged down to the cellar beneath the family home. There, by the hands of those meant to love and protect her, she was tied to a dirty mattress and gagged so she could not speak or shout out about the horrors that were beginning to unfold: Rosemary began to act out her twisted sexual fantasies on the girl, first whispering loving words to her, then fondling and tearing her vagina, and then thrusting a vibrator into her small body. As if that wasn't a horror enough, her father then brutally raped her, all the while keeping up the facade of whispering sweet and loving words to her.

'Everybody does it to every girl,' Rosemary told Anne Marie. 'It's a father's job. Don't worry, and don't say anything to anybody.'

It is impossible to imagine the mixture of horror and confusion for a little girl whose sister and mother had disappeared and who was now at the mercy of her father and his new and much younger partner who verbally gave all the signals of being kind and nurturing while committing acts of horror beyond anyone's imagination.

The only last shred of hope would be that this insane incident was the end of it, that Rosemary West and her depraved husband woke up the next morning steeped in the deepest sense of shame that their macabre sexual fantasies had got the better of them.

But that was far from how it played out.

The sexual violation of such a small child was soon knitted into everyday life at 25 Cromwell Street, along with all the other twisted things taking place, and it was only going to get worse and worse as their appetite for depravity grew.

It's likely that Anne Marie was the first of all the victims to be abused there, and it did not take long before the couple treated her entire existence and body as nothing more than a resource for their sexual pleasure, and that of others.

Sometimes when they raped her, they said she should be grateful and that they were 'helping' her. They would comfort her and stroke her hair afterwards, even run her a bath with bath salts. Then the sadism and torture began again, and soon enough, they were offering her up to other 'clients' visiting the house, the paedophiles of Gloucester who now had a one-stop shop where they could have sex with an innocent young girl under the same roof as her parents, and with their knowledge and approval.

Fred's brother John also began arriving at the house to have his fantasies fulfilled, and to give a sense of the life – and nightmare – that Anne Marie was living is the fact that she estimates that her so-called Uncle John raped her more than three hundred times from the time she was eight until she ran away from the house at age fifteen.

Fred began to treat the habitual rape of his eldest daughter as a hobby. He even fashioned instruments of torture to use on her, and she was forced to sometimes walk around or do the dishes with a vibrator inserted inside her vagina.

It's as if Anne Marie were living as a hostage with Stockholm syndrome, but her captors were her own father and stepmother. She also didn't know that her mother and sister were dead, and though one might imagine she felt abandoned by them, thinking they had simply stopped contacting her, instead she was more fearful that they were upset with her for still living with Fred.

Anne Marie did make a few half-hearted attempts to contact her mother Rena but she always seemed to back off at the last minute. 'She was scared that her mother would reject her and tell her "You chose to go off with your father. It's your bloody problem,"' explained Chris, who would later become her first husband. She had a pathological fear of rejection, as it was something that she had experienced her whole life.

Her two younger siblings were still tiny, and so it was that Anne Marie was living a nightmare with nobody to turn to for help. Even if one imagined the habitual rape taken out of the equation, it is difficult to imagine the strange world she was living in.

As a sensitive child who lived in survival mode 24 hours a day, she would have been finely attuned to the sounds of the house: men traipsing up and down the stairs at all hours of the day and night; the comforting sounds of lodgers coming and going, living normal lives; and the terror of hearing Fred and Rosemary opening the door of her room to visit horrors upon her.

This child, with a broken spirit, soon realised that lodgers at the house must have been able to hear her when she let out screams of pain in the middle of the night. She knew this because she overheard them asking her parents about it. But when the Wests simply dismissed the sounds as just another of their daughter's nightmares, no further questions from the lodgers were forthcoming.

The presence of so many young people drifting through the house could have provided a lifeline to Anne Marie. One particular young woman, Gill Britt, walked through the doors of the house and became a symbol of a life outside of which Anne Marie could only dream for her own future.

Gill was seventeen years old and full of the joys of youth. She was immersed in the growing punk scene of the seventies and was travelling to gigs by bands like The Clash and the Sex Pistols all over the country. She would later recall how she played her records extra loudly on her record player to cover up the sounds that would come from the West household above and below. She would hear Rosemary shouting, screaming and swearing, calling the children 'fucking bitches', or chasing them around inside the house before the sounds of sobs would soon reverberate.

In contrast, Fred, as monstrous as he was, never seemed to raise his voice loud enough to be overheard by Gill. She later recalled how he seemed to share her concerns about his wife.

'Sometimes you'd look at Fred if you heard Rose shouting and his eyes would go up in his head, and he would just walk away. He was quite aware that she was screaming and moaning and using obscene language,' she would later recall.

Gill also got a glimpse into the repugnant personality of 'Uncle John', who was raping little Anne Marie, his niece, so often.

He was a foreboding presence in the house, and on one occasion, Britt went down to make a payment to Fred and found him sitting with his brother John. She stayed and chatted for a while until John suddenly pushed her up against the wall and said to Fred, 'So what are we going to do with this one, hey Fred?' The incident only lasted a few seconds but Britt recalled feeling scared and powerless, and she made a conscious decision in that moment to never put herself in a position where she was alone with John. In contrast, Anne Marie had no agency over anything in her life, and being raped by this same man was just another fact of her wretched life – as was being forced to perform household chores while wearing a mini skirt with the vibrator inside her, being tied to furniture, or contracting syphilis from her own father when she was still a child.

This was all against a backdrop of utterly strange things being normalised in the household. For example, the house was always strewn with sex toys and extremely graphic pornography, not the least of which were magazines that advertised Rosemary's sexual services. The Wests had also amassed a large collection of bondage and restraining devices, sexual fetish magazines and photographs, later expanding this collection to include videos depicting bestiality and graphic sexual abuse of children.

Her life was so subverted to her parents' monstrous behaviour, and she was so gaslit by them into thinking this was what normality looked like, that she did not have the mental strength to seek help outside the home.

Once or twice, she did so within the home, but no help was forthcoming. There was one day when she made her way to the section of the house where the West children seldom wandered. She knocked on lodger Gill's door and asked gingerly if she could come inside. Gill was getting ready to go out on the town for a night of fun, but she said Anne Marie could sit with her while she got ready.

'Look what they make me do,' Gill later recalled Anne Marie saying over and over. She was still in her school clothes, and she pulled her shirt down to reveal the top of her torso. She showed Gill a series of black bruises on her chest and on her breast, and Gill remembers thinking that they were 'horrific'. Anne Marie made it quite clear they were not self-inflicted wounds and that there were other people who were doing this to her, including her 'mother' Rose.

The lodger was horrified by what she saw, but she was just a teenager herself and perhaps unaware of the magnitude of what the young girl was trying to tell her. Her only strategy was to try and soothe Anne Marie with platitudes about a better future after she turned sixteen. She failed to listen closely to what Anne Marie was saying and didn't try to intervene. She would later say that there was also no Childline at the time, and less sophisticated systems were in place to stop domestic violence and child abuse.

This encounter with Gill was just one of many potential, but failed, lifelines for Anne Marie, who was stuck in the vicious cycle of abuse against a backdrop of seeming – and at moments – even genuine normality, making life very confusing.

Alongside the grotesque lack of sexual inhibitions and the violence, which included intermittent kicks in the face from her father in his steel-toe-capped shoes, there were a few little moments when Anne Marie got a slight sense of what a normal family might be like. For example, Rose was known to bake 'superb' iced cakes for her birthday, and sometimes Anne Marie (and later her siblings) received Christmas presents bought from the Argos catalogue. There were even one or two camping holidays during which no sexual violence took place.

But in the larger picture, life was as warped as it could be. In 1979, when the rape had been going on for seven years and Anne Marie was fifteen years old, she fell pregnant. This must have been one of the strangest times in a household where 'strange' was of an extreme few others would be able to fathom.

Anne Marie was pregnant by her father, and at the same time, Rosemary was pregnant by a client. Also around that time, a young lodger at the house, Shirley Robinson, who was in love with Fred and having an ongoing affair with him, was also pregnant.

As fate would have it, Anne Marie's pregnancy would prove to be very complicated. As if she had not had enough trauma and physical pain in her life, she now found herself writhing around on a bed with severe abdominal pain. This was followed by profuse vaginal bleeding, which got so bad that Fred and Rosemary decided they had no choice but to take her to a hospital. This, despite their wanting to keep the whole sordid situation under wraps.

The doctors examined Anne Marie and discovered that the pregnancy was ectopic. In other words, the fertilised egg had begun to develop not inside the uterus but in one of the fallopian tubes. That is always an extremely dangerous situation for a pregnant woman, as it was for Anne Marie, the pregnant child.

And so, under the bright light of an operating table, Anne Marie West was anaesthetised while the surgeon made an incision in her abdomen to remove the growing foetus from her tube, a foetus of a child whose father was also her grandfather.

When Anne Marie returned from hospital, still in pain from an invasive operation and the confusion of having had a dangerous pregnancy terminated, all she needed was some care and sympathy. Instead, she was met with a furious Rosemary who gave her a savage beating, including a hard punch in the stomach.

This was some type of final straw for a girl who had endured many lifetimes of violence, grief and sexual abuse in her short fifteen years. She first had to recover from the physical pain of the operation, but as soon as she felt well enough, she secretly packed her small suitcase, with which she had walked through the doors of this same house seven years prior, and headed out onto the streets to fend for herself.

With no sense of self-worth, no resources, and no adults who truly cared about her, she made the best plan she could and found a dingy room to rent above a lowbrow pub. The only person in the world she could trust was a boy called Chris Davis, whom she had been dating even when she lived at the house in Cromwell Street. He moved into the room with her, and for the first time in her life, she might have felt vaguely safe.

What did play on her mind, however, was being caught by the police after running away from home instead of waiting until she was sixteen. It was a real testimony to her toxic upbringing that she felt that she, rather than her father and stepmother, had done something wrong and should fear the actions of the police.

Chris was a lifeline for Anne Marie in those days, and she felt safe enough to share her story with him. On hearing the grim details of all that had befallen her, he was outraged and was determined to do something about it.

But she begged him not to. As had been the story of her own life, she did not want what she had endured to be out there in the world, and she began to panic. Her argument was this: 'They will kill you and then they will kill me.'

But as time went on, Chris and Anne Marie started to run out of options. It wasn't too long before their meagre savings were gone; they could not pay the rent and Anne Marie was forced to go back home again, a decision that must have been absolute torture for her. Before they returned home, they made a plan to spend as little time as possible there in the company of her parents, and in the months that followed and with the hovering presence of her boyfriend, she finally seemed to manage to create some distance from her family home.

With Anne Marie inching away from him, Fred filled the void in his soul by turning his unwelcome attention onto the next two girls, whom he had complete control over – Heather and Mae.

8

Two More Killings

By 1978, Juanita Mott's sisters still had no sign of her. Hopes had also dimmed for the families of the other girls who had vanished – Lynda, Carole Ann, Therese and Lucy. But for Rosemary and Fred West, living at 25 Cromwell Street with their children, the facade of normal life and a culture of 'minding your own business' threw a veil over their dark secrets. For three years, as far as is known, they had not been out on the prowl looking for new victims and dragging them down into the cellar.

Now, Fred was busier than ever, running around town with his van full of handyman tools. He picked up jobs wherever he could and intermittently found seasonal work in the factories of Gloucester or on construction sites. Rosemary, for her part, was still running her one-woman brothel in Mandy's room upstairs at the family home and screaming and swearing at her three children.

Like other Britons, Rosemary and Fred probably felt they could breathe a little easier with the worst of the country's recession behind them – despite the still high unemployment – and the inflation rate having come down.

In that same year, 1978, Fred hatched a plan to lay a new concrete floor down in the cellar and turn it into a bedroom for his children – or so he told the neighbours. There he stood in front of the rows of semis in Cromwell Street, mixing up a thick grey cement while making idle conversation with other residents in the street who came and went.

'I'm doing my own renovations,' he would tell them, boasting about the financial rewards he would reap and the value he was adding. His plan was to move the girls down into the basement and, in so doing, free up their bedroom so they could generate revenue from even more lodgers.

The idea behind this likely came from Rose, who firmly controlled the family purse strings. On Fridays, Fred would arrive home sweaty from a week's work and hand over his cash to her. She would add it to what she made from prostitution and decide how it would be budgeted.

Over those years, a lot of the money flowed into makeshift house alterations as the semi-detached creaked under the strain of a growing family, lodgers streaming in and out, and Rosemary's clients who had come for sex.

The years between 1973 and 1978 represented one of the longest extended periods of Rosemary's childbearing age during which she wasn't pregnant. Stephen, born in 1973, looked to be the last born, though that was all about to change.

Her parents, Bill and Daisy, were still present in Rosemary's life. The memories from all those years ago, when they were outraged at her relationship with Fred, were over. Rosemary was now 26 and, unbeknownst to her mother, she was still having sex with her own father. Yes, she had grown up and moved away, but the little girl who had been repeatedly raped was now hosting her father in Mandy's room from time to time, the same place where she entertained all her other clients.

Unlike when she was a child, Rose now had full agency over her sexuality, but the question always lingered as to whether Bill was the root of all this evil and why she would still be having sex with him.

And so, the man who had broken her virginity when she was a child was now traipsing up the same stairs as her many clients, in the same house where his four grandchildren lived and where his son-in-law made it clear that this ongoing incest had his blessing. Why wouldn't it? He, too, was raping his own offspring, and his wife having sex with anyone else was a thrill for him. Perhaps the only difference between Bill and Rose's other clients was that in the case of the former, Fred was not standing with his cold blue eyes pressed to the wall where the peepholes had been drilled.

Fred and his father-in-law had a strange relationship at the best of times. By 1977, Bill had developed a grudging respect for the man he had once hated and, bizarrely, might have also felt relieved that he had Fred's blessing to carry on having sex with his daughter.

He and Daisy were now living above a dingy pub called the Green Lantern Cafe on Southgate Street, Gloucester, just five minutes away from Rose and Fred. One day, when Bill saw the 'For Sale' sign outside the pub, he let his son-in-law know it was on the market. Shortly after this, Fred made a business decision that was very much out of character: he decided to put in a joint offer with Bill to buy the place.

Fred, who had once driven an ice cream van and then an abattoir truck before earning his meagre wage through manual labour in the construction industry, now fancied himself as a pub owner and landlord. It is also entirely likely that at this stage, the pub represented more than just a business opportunity. It was also the perfect honey trap in which he could meet young girls whose lives he and Rosemary could destroy.

On a spring day in 1978, Fred was at the Green Lantern when a young woman just shy of twenty years of age walked through the doors. With feathered black hair and dark eyes, Shirley Robinson had a worldliness about her that few other young women had – she had lived some of her life abroad, and the influence of Europe on her outlook was clear.

She had been born in Leicester to a British father, who was a member of the Royal Air Force, and a German mother. The RAF maintained a significant presence in West Germany during the Cold War years, and though little is known about Shirley's childhood, she might have been one of the many children who were born to RAF parents who settled in the territory for a while during this period. These families typically lived in purpose-built accommodation on or near the base. They were usually quite close-knit communities with their own schools, shops, medical facilities, and social clubs, and the children of service members attended British Forces schools on base, following the UK curriculum.

It is likely that Shirley spent at least a portion of her childhood in this safe and protected way, but after her parents split up, her fortunes took a turn for the worse.

She moved back to the UK, where she lived in the West Midlands. Like so many other children at the time, her life fell apart after the divorce, and when hard decisions had to be made, she found her security upended as she was forced to live in child protective custody.

Shirley's change in circumstances had brought on a level of desperation, and she now turned to the one resource she had to earn a living: her body.

This meant having to grow up rather quickly to fend for herself, and it was during this hard period that she stepped through the doors of the Green Lantern Cafe, looking for a break from walking the streets.

As a worldly, street-smart teenager, she made an immediate impression on Fred, who was only too pleased when they got chatting about her hunt for cheap accommodation.

Fred, of course, knew just the place that would suit her needs and told her it was only a convenient five-minute walk away.

She accepted his offer on the spot, and less than a week later, Shirley Robinson knocked on the door of 25 Cromwell Street, clutching her meagre possessions and counting her blessings that she'd had the fortune of meeting a pub owner who also had a house with affordable rooms.

It did not take long before Fred was more than just a landlord to Shirley. Within a few weeks, a romantic and sexual relationship had formed between the two. Shirley was only nineteen at the time, and Fred was now 37. It is possible that their sexual relationship also involved Rosemary, as group sex and threesomes was a defining feature of Fred and Rose's marriage. However, at some point, Rose, who was 25 years old by then, began to look on in jealous suspicion at their growing affections.

By September of 1977, Shirley was pregnant with Fred's child, while his wife Rosemary was pregnant with the child of a client of her sex work.

This configuration was a far cry from the scenario of previous years in which Rosemary and Fred would trawl the streets looking for any young woman waiting at a bus stop or hitching a lift. Although this domestic set-up was bizarre, it didn't stop Rose from boasting at first to the neighbours about her pregnant lodger.

Shirley, for her part, now living in the house and pregnant with the child of the 'man of the house', had begun to imagine a future with Fred West as her husband. One day, she sat down with pen and paper to write to her father in Germany, announcing to him that she was in love, pregnant, and planning to get married.

Inside the envelope, she tucked a photograph of her with the man she was telling her father would be his future son-in-law. In that photograph, Shirley has all the sparkle of a girl of nineteen in her eyes. Her hair is cut in a feathered style typical of the era, and Fred is standing next to her in a blue tie and patterned grey tweed jacket.

It is heartbreaking to imagine how oblivious she was to the fact that the man she held so closely in that image had already raped and murdered so many people, and that his wife, whose friendship was quickly turning to hatred, was just as monstrous.

Rosemary's feelings towards Shirley began to curdle when the threat loomed of her being a replacement in Fred's life. Everyone knew that the father of the child was Fred, and even Fred's own mother found out about it.

But Fred, not one for owning up to his misdemeanours, flatly denied it to his mother and insisted he had only ever been in love with his second wife, Rose.

Shirley had little idea of the depth of Rosemary's relationship with her husband and the twisted history that bonded them together. Accounts of Rosemary's public persona at the time describe her as having a childlike demeanour, with the clothes to match. Shirley likely encountered this too, while also seeing a different picture painted by how Rosemary treated her children, screaming and swearing at them as she did.

Either way, young Shirley, whose life had been torn to shreds by her parents' divorce, now imagined that she had landed in a place of financial and emotional safety, and the more she relaxed into the homestead, the more Rose treated her as an existential threat.

The teenager was blissfully unaware that she had shifted in Rose's eyes from being just another lover to being the enemy that would need to be removed.

And soon enough, in the summer of 1977, Shirley Robinson, with her beautiful face and belly swollen with an eight-month pregnancy, disappeared off the face of the earth.

And, a few weeks later, Rose turned up at the offices of the Gloucester social services. 'I am here to collect maternity benefits on behalf of Shirley Robinson,' she told the clerk behind the wooden desk.

In the days and weeks that followed, a few people asked about Shirley. They had, after all, been told the exciting news of her pregnancy and had chatted to her as neighbours do on the pavements of Cromwell Street.

But when asked where Shirley was and how she was doing and if the baby was due any day soon, Rose simply returned to her tried and tested playbook that had satisfied those who'd asked after Charmaine and Lynda all those years ago: Shirley had decided to relocate. The story, this time, was that the pregnant lodger simply upped and left to live with her father in West Germany and that that was the last anyone had heard from her.

***

As always, Fred and Rose resumed life as they knew it. Little Tara was born, meaning that Rosemary, at the age of 25, now had five children in her care, and the twisted dichotomy of 25 Cromwell Street continued: part domestic life, part hypersexual playground for a couple with a macabre taste for twisted sexual fantasies.

It was barely a year later when Alison Chambers arrived on the scene with a background very similar to that of Shirley.

She was born on 8 September 1962 in Hanover, West Germany, where her father was serving in the RAF. Just like Shirley, she moved back to the UK when she was young, but unlike Shirley, she found herself living in Swansea, on the south coast of Wales.

However, for reasons that are not recorded, she moved into a children's home in Gloucester, a hundred miles away, though it is possible she had run away from home.

As she slowly got used to institutional life, she enrolled in a youth training scheme, and it was under this banner that she found work in a firm of solicitors. But, as fate would have it, she also attended the same school as Anne Marie West, and the two girls became friends, with Anne Marie seemingly the only person who had time for the naive and lonely Alison.

Not unexpectedly, Anne Marie began inviting her around to the house to visit – two outcast teenage girls looking for friendship in the context of a troubled life.

As Alison became a frequent visitor to the house, Rosemary would butter her up by telling her she could relate exactly to what Alison had already been through in her short life and understood her feelings about life being difficult.

She went so far as to give Alison a little fake gold necklace with her name on it, and she showed her a picture of a farm she said she and Fred owned. She reassured Alison that life would get better and that she could move into their so-called farmhouse once she moved out of Jordan's Brook House.

Were it not for the tragic fate that awaited her, Alison as a youngster would likely have slipped into obscurity and never been written about in any shape or form. It would later fall to the lodger Gill Britt to recall what she could of this young woman.

Gill remembered her as having 'a very fashionable, but mousey, Farrah Fawcett style hairdo'.

Certainly, her life was the polar opposite of Farrah Fawcett's, whose role in the popular TV show *Charlie's Angels* made her one of the most admired and recognisable women of the decade.

TWO MORE KILLINGS

Alison, on the other hand, was known by very few and understood by even fewer. And so, in her search for someone to care for her, she clung tightly to Gill Britt, who was simply a little older and who had taken a bit of interest in her life. Not long after they met, she started sending Gill loving letters as if Gill were a relative or close friend.

She was also somewhat rebellious, and perhaps, as a bit of a lost soul, she just wanted more than anything to be noticed. Her friends described her as someone who needed a fair amount of attention.

There are few details about the life she was living in the children's home, but it was unlikely to have been very nurturing, and just before her seventeenth birthday, she packed up her bags and quietly walked out of the doors of the place that was, at the very least, giving her three square meals a day and a bed to sleep in.

She also gave up her work as a secretary, and perhaps it was with more than just a sense of excitement when she knocked on the door of the house where she would start her first day as a live-in nanny – 25 Cromwell Street, Gloucester.

Little did she know that she was the latest in a long line of vulnerable girls that started all the way back with Anne McFall over a decade earlier.

In a letter to her mother, which in retrospect contains heartbreaking details of how she felt this was all going to pan out, she wrote, 'I am living with a very homely family.' She added, 'I look after their five children and do some of their housework. They also have a child the same age as me who accepts me as a big sister, and we get on great. The family owns flats, and I share with the oldest sister.'

She told her mum 'not to worry' about her, as she was doing just fine in this cosy domestic set-up.

But Rosemary West and her lecherous husband, with the gap in the teeth and the wiry black hair, knew just how to manipulate someone like Alison Chambers with her big, bright eyes and neat eyebrows.

She likely took them as a surrogate family, enjoying the attention and gifts that came her way. At some point, however, she began to describe Fred to others as an older man who was very much in love with her.

And then, just like that, she vanished.

The Wests' knack of preying on vulnerable young women ensured that the police force hardly took notice when they went missing. These were not families like the Partingtons or the Goughs who began desperate manhunts and badgered the police. These were young women who, at the best of times, were treated as a nuisance by the system.

And so, when Alison Chambers vanished and was reported missing, the police took one look at her history and filed it away under A for abscondment. This was nothing more than a young girl having run away from a children's home. Case closed.

If Shirley Hubbard's disappearance a year before was the end result of a jealous Rosemary eliminating a threat, that of Alison Chambers was more of a grim throwback to the Wests' modus operandi from years before.

It then begs the question of whether the Wests had been carrying out their perverted actions in those intervening years but hiding the 'evidence' at a different location.

9

Heather's Gone

Like her sister Anne Marie before her, Heather West was counting down the days to her sixteenth birthday. Only then could she legally break free from the shackles of a home where her mother beat and belittled her, her father raped her, and she bore witness to her youngster siblings enduring the same cycles of violence over and over again.

School life, often her only escape from the workings of the family home, was where Heather found at least some footing. Though she was considered strange by the other pupils as she withdrew further and further into herself, she was a bright student with an excellent attendance record. Each morning, no matter what horrors had unfolded the night before, she would be dressed neat as a pin in her white school blouse and dark navy tie and jumper, with an eighties haircut neatly combed for the school day ahead.

And it was this exact uniform that helped her hide her bruised body from the world. Classmates would later recall that Heather never wanted to change in front of anyone when they had to swap school clothes for sports kits, and that on one occasion when Heather did shower at school, others looked on in horror at the map of bruises and welts all over her body.

But of course, she had a story ready. These bruises, she claimed, were from playful fighting with her siblings.

Arriving home from school each day was like playing the slot machines at a casino. She might find Rose faking the role of the normal mum, or she might find herself being kicked and slapped, verbally abused and accused of being 'a lesbian'. In the deep homophobia of the era, this was Rose's attempt at insulting her daughter for resisting her father's sexual advances.

The barely literate Fred, meanwhile, kept a record of Heather's menstrual cycle. Perhaps he had finally realised that a little awareness about cycles could prevent another daughter from getting pregnant with his child. For her, it was just one more in a long list of reasons why she dreamed of being alone in the forest, away from the madness of her family.

She took to going around barefoot and dreaming of a life in the forest away from any and all prying eyes, but this attempt to detach from her grim reality was accompanied by a deep state of depression that saw her staring into space and lacking any energy.

Her power-hungry parents detested her yearning for freedom and wanted to break her spirit as much as they wanted to hurt her body. And the more she tried to prevent her father from raping her, the more enraged he became.

Not surprisingly, all men came to symbolise the horrors she was going through at home. She regarded the male teachers at her school as a threat and told the principal she could not attend any classes that a man was taking.

The school responded at first by suspending her for making this unusual request, but later acquiesced and ensured all her teachers going forward were only female. What's heartbreaking, in light of what followed, is the fact that the principal, like so many adults before, did not probe the situation to find out exactly why she had made this request in the first place.

***

In the spring of 1987, Heather's dreams came true for one brief moment. She and her classmates from Hucclecote Secondary School, since demolished, stood outside the building with their bags packed for a camping trip. Off they headed to Heather's favourite place, the Forest of Dean, where the beauty of nature stood in such sharp contrast to the horror of her life at home with her parents. For two weeks, Heather experienced what her heart had always needed – the fresh water of a river flowing over rocks, the crunch of leaves beneath her bare feet, and all the sounds and the taste of fresh air in the forest. She saw creatures of the forest – pine martens, deer, woodpeckers and foxes – living the kind of carefree life she could only dream about.

The days sped by too quickly for Heather, who had soaked up the freedom away from Fred and Rose. When the trip was over, even those who had enjoyed it were excited to be heading home, and all gathered at the spot where the transport would arrive. One by one, they filed onto the bus, but one person was missing: Heather West was nowhere to be found. She had wandered off on her own deep into the woods with no intention of returning to 25 Cromwell Street. A search party was then hastily put together to comb through the forest, and there they found Heather, resisting the trip back into Gloucester with all her might.

But like everyone else, she finally stepped onto the bus and headed home, and it was shortly after this taste of freedom that she began to confide in her friend Denise about the horrors that were unfolding at her house. She told Denise about the cruel sexual and physical violence that was taking place behind closed doors. Denise was shaken and told her parents what was happening to her best friend, but they were unsure of what to do about it and hesitated to report it to the authorities. Yet another possible moment that could have changed Heather's fate slipped by and was gone.

On 17 June 1987, Heather put on a baggy white T-shirt and some leggings. Withdrawn and depressed, she was in no mood for a party, but her older sister Anne Marie had invited the family over to celebrate her daughter Michelle's third birthday. Heather made the two-mile journey to her sister's place but the two of them got no time together. Anne Marie was focused on giving Michelle a great birthday party and had invited many guests with whom she had to mingle. Heather, for her part, stood sullen and quiet at the bottom of the garden, her long dark hair hanging loose over her shoulders. She did not interact with the children squealing with delight around her, and she was too withdrawn to make conversation with any of the adults.

One of the mothers at the party overheard Fred reprimanding Heather for 'standing around like a fucking lemon', while Heather responded with a request to be 'left a-fucking-lone'. Too depressed to manage the social milieu of the gathering, Heather let herself out by the small gate at the bottom of the garden that led into the street and walked home, dreaming about finding a way to escape.

Later that night, the phone rang at 25 Cromwell Street, and it was Anne Marie who told Fred that one of the mothers at the party had complained about Heather swearing. When Fred hung up the phone, he grabbed hold of Heather and gave her a savage beating for drawing so much attention to herself. Heather felt betrayed by her older sister for telling their dad and vowed never to speak to her again.

She was also, or so she believed, about to cast off the shackles of her heinous home life. After briefly considering joining the army, she had instead applied for a job as a maid at the Butlins Holiday Camp in the seaside town of Torquay in Devon, 120 miles away.

There she would be tasked with cleaning chalets and would be surrounded by families playing in the waterparks, watching live entertainment and relaxing at restaurants – in other words, families having the type of normal fun she had never known.

But the night before she was meant to leave, which was also the night after Michelle's third birthday, she received a call saying the job had fallen through. In that single moment, Heather went from believing her nightmare would finally be over to realising that she was stuck in the dark web that her parents had spun around her.

Mae would later recall how Heather sobbed through the night. She was inconsolable, and even her sister who had been with her through thick and thin had never witnessed her feeling quite so defeated.

The following morning, 19 June 1987, a big summer rainfall was pelting down on Gloucester. Heather, still heartbroken about the job falling through, watched quietly as her younger siblings got dressed for school and headed out.

Fred was busy on a job at the time, but the rain meant he too would be at home on this particular day. It was a Friday, and Heather would have liked nothing better than to see her father head off. The system that she, Mae and Stephen had developed to make sure none of them was ever alone with Fred had worked up to a point, but now, thanks to the rain, Heather would be at home alone with both Fred and her mother.

And, not surprisingly, it wasn't long before Fred and Rose picked a fight with their daughter, whose spirit they had already crushed so hard. All Rose would later admit to a neighbour who had overheard the fight was that 'yes, there was a hell of a row'.

***

Later that day, a garbage truck trundled along the road that leads down to St Michael's Square in Gloucester. The dustbin man, like on any other day, lifted and emptied the detritus from the bins into the back of the truck that squeezed through the narrow roads of the square. What he would not have known is that all the precious belongings and the clothes that a girl of sixteen had chosen to wear on a rainy day in the summer of 1987 were now lying among the restaurant leftovers and retail packaging from the square, where the police would never find them. They would end up in a landfill, buried just like the secrets of what happened in this home of extreme abuse.

In the late afternoon, around 5 p.m., Mae and Stephen returned from school after a long week. It was Friday, and, exhausted as they plonked their school bags down and turned on the TV, they expected to find their older sister Heather sitting there in the family section of the house as she always did.

But Heather was nowhere to be seen.

Little Stephen asked, 'Where's Heather?'

Fred, as matter of fact as ever, replied, 'She's left home.'

The children's risk radar went on high alert. 'What do you mean?' asked Mae and Stephen, whose every move up to this point in their lives had been in relation to Heather and their pact to never be apart when the parents were around.

In a cruel twist of irony, Fred now invoked the very summer camp that Heather had longed to work at to escape from her mother and father.

He told the two younger siblings that the woman from Butlins had called back to say Heather did get the job after all, and she had immediately packed her bags. He embellished the story with more detail to give it an air of authenticity and added that a woman in a Mini had arrived to whisk her away to camp. Stephen and Mae were happy for their sister but surprised that she would have left without a note.

But later, Stephen found one of Heather's most prized possessions, a book she had won at school for her achievements.

He was perplexed, but he was too young to ask the right questions, or more likely, he was terrified of the beating he'd get if he asked any questions at all. The same went for Mae. She too knew better than to raise the ire of their volatile mother or unpredictable father, who had already caused them enough misery for a lifetime.

And so, the children were forced to accept that their sister had gone off to work at a summer camp and had not said goodbye. That night, the two of them crawled into bed in the cellar, keenly aware of the absence of their older sister.

At that time, Mae had just turned fifteen and Stephen was fourteen, and the two teenagers listened quietly as their parents told the extended family that Heather had gone to work at summer camp.

Just a few days after she had vanished from the family home, Fred called his only son and handed him a spade, instructing him to dig a deep hole in the garden.

He said he had decided to build a fish pond and that he wanted the newly dug hole to be 'four feet deep and six across'.

'I want you to lay blue plastic in the hole and leave it,' he added.

It was the half-term break, and young Stephen went about obeying his father's instructions. He might have been slightly perplexed that his father suddenly wanted a fish pond in the small garden out the back of the semi, but in a house where anything strange was entirely possible, he had no reason to be suspicious of his father's instructions. Stephen got to work and dug the hole.

But a few days later, expecting to see the fish pond coming to fruition, he instead saw all his hard work undone. Fred had filled it in with soil once again and now announced he wanted to build a patio on the spot.

Not long after that, some huge Innsworth patio slabs were lugged through the West household and laid down neatly across the back garden by Fred himself. And then, in a final flourish of setting the stage of a normal family living in a semi in Gloucester, Fred built a barbecue area and placed a pine table and chairs over the newly built patio.

Stephen forgot about the strange fish pond instructions and embraced the new area. They all did. As the summer holidays unfolded, the Wests took to having barbecues out the back on the new patio like a normal family: Rose cooking up burgers and frying bacon, music pumping out from a speaker by the kitchen window, Fred with his gap-toothed grin moving about the garden and chatting with the neighbours and lodgers.

With little to no information about the whereabouts of their sister, other than the narrative of her being 'a cleaner at summer camp', Mae and Stephen expected her to return when the holiday drew to a close.

But by the time they went back to school, there was still no sign of Heather. And even when the warm summer days gave way to the cooler nights of autumn, their big sister still had not come home or made any contact. This, after not even saying goodbye, began to strike them as odd.

They now could not hold back and started asking their parents repeatedly where Heather was and why she never called. The parents realised they needed to do something and so now changed their story. Heather had not actually gone to work as a cleaner at the summer camp. She had in fact come out as a lesbian and had run away with her female lover, who had come to pick her up, and they wanted nothing more to do with her.

A neighbour was told Heather had 'run away' shortly after the big row the neighbour had heard on that fateful morning.

But Mae and Stephen were still confused as to why their big sister, who had loved them so much and been in a trio of protection with them down in that cellar, was now making no effort to contact them. Anne Marie was also beside herself with worry about Heather, especially after all her inquiries came to nothing. She also felt dreadful about the last time she had seen her sister and how they had barely spoken at the birthday party.

All three of the children become suspicious that something had happened, but not of their own parents.

'We should report her disappearance to the police,' Mae told Fred and Rose.

But now the parents changed the story yet again to explain away their decision not to do this. Heather, they now said, was involved in credit card fraud and alerting the police would work against her, so it was best to keep it under wraps.

They augmented all these fake stories by pretending, from time to time, that she had phoned. They even persuaded someone, perhaps Fred's brother John, who knew so many of their secrets, to call the family at home and pretend to be Heather, and on more than one occasion, Fred would arrive home at 25 Cromwell Street and announce to Heather's confused siblings that he had seen her out and about in other towns in the region.

But perhaps most poignant of all is the fact that when Heather had first disappeared from the family home a week after her final school day, it was just two days before the school results came out.

When the results were announced, the bright child, who had endured every type of horror under the roof of her family home and had got up each morning for school despite the odds, had achieved eight GCSEs and, under very different circumstances, would have had a whole promising life ahead of her.

Instead, she had not even lived to hear the news of how all her hard work had paid off.

10

Missed Opportunities

Life for the West family settled back into some kind of routine after Heather had, in the eyes of her siblings, mysteriously disappeared without saying goodbye. For Rose, who was entering her late thirties, and Fred, who was approaching fifty, their daughter's death was no big milestone that would alter the landscape of their daily lives.

He still worked long hours as a handyman or a builder, driving all over the country to work on construction sites and sending his wages back for Rose to manage just as meticulously as she did her bookings for her clients.

Mandy's room was still a hive of activity, and life in the house continued as it always had: a bizarre mixture of the ordinariness of domestic life, set against a backdrop of unimaginable violence and abuse.

Anne Marie's obsession with finding her missing sister and following every lead she could finally gave way to a heartbreaking realisation that she may never know the truth. Not a day had gone by that she hadn't been worried sick about her sister, but now there was nothing to do but carry on raising her own family. Heather, like Charmaine and her mother Rena, became yet another loved one that haunted her dreams but never showed up in real life.

Anne Marie was also weighed down by the anxiety, as were Mae and Stephen, that some of the younger children still caught in the dark world of life at 25 Cromwell Street were getting to the age where Fred and his brother, Uncle John, would be preying on them to satisfy their own paedophiliac hunger. Rose, for her part, was still every bit the volcano in the house, and though she erupted less frequently during this period, she was still a grave threat to the infants and pubescent youngsters in her care.

It is difficult to say whether Rose and Fred felt any differently about the murder of their own child than they did about anyone else who'd had the misfortune of crossing their path, but one thing seems certain: they thought they'd got away with it, and that the web of lies surrounding Heather's disappearance had shut the mouths of those asking too many questions.

Two whole decades had passed between Anne McFall and the unborn baby in her belly falling victim to Fred's brutal hands and Rose and Fred's daughter Heather meeting the same fate. And over that time, more than a dozen young girls and women had gone missing but not a single person with pen, paper and a police badge had joined the dots.

To the authorities, these were cold cases. In other instances, nobody had even reported anyone missing. And so, far from living in fear of a knock on the door from the authorities, Rose and Fred simply went about their daily lives, Rose prostituting herself upstairs in Mandy's room, Fred doing his construction work, and a brood of children living under their roof in blind fear of the next beating.

What remains one of the most baffling aspects of the gruesome story is the number of times anyone with half an eye or interest could have figured out what was happening and put a stop to it.

In hindsight, their lives together were lit up with warning signs at every turn. Of course, at the time, police technology was less sophisticated, digital records did not exist, making it harder to join the dots, and socioeconomic class divisions also, albeit unofficially, dictated the extent to which the authorities paid attention. But even so, the police's inability to take heed of those warning signs and make the connection is staggering.

This is true not only of the murders, but also of Fred's predilection for sexual violence, tracing all the way back to the violation of his younger sister Kitty.

***

Today, popular cultural forms from movies to podcasts are obsessed with fictitious and true crime and the psychological profile of those who commit it, especially if it's as cold-blooded as serial killing. Against this backdrop, it would be tempting to imagine Rose and Fred as being sophisticated criminal masterminds who were able to evade the law through sheer savvy and perfect planning.

This, however, would not only be a false narrative but would betray the victims and their families, many of whom would not have lost their lives or loved ones had the system been more efficient.

It was not the brain power behind Rose and Fred that kept them out of the limelight of a policeman's torch. It was, instead, a string of failures on the part of so many different entities, a few strokes of 'luck' on the part of Rose and Fred, or, as some have claimed, a case of the right palms being greased at the right time.

The police had failed miserably at joining the dots, spotting patterns and looking in the right places. But added to this were the failings of social services, the education system, the medical staff at hospitals, the caregivers in children's homes – the list goes on. It is possible none were in a position to identify the repeated modus operandi within a bigger picture, and yet, even in the absence of digital records, it would not have taken much to trace more than one of the missing girls back to Rosemary and Fred West.

Charmaine's disappearance in the 'early' days is a case in point, bearing in mind that she and her sister had been placed into care five times between 1965 and 1970. When Charmaine disappeared for good, the school she attended was told that she had returned to her biological mother, Rena, and the school took it at face value. Not a single other inquiry was made. If they had tried to verify this, a red flag might have popped up when they couldn't trace the said mother (Rena had been dead for two years), and if this had caused any suspicion, the testimony of the little girl who witnessed Charmaine being beaten while tied to a chair would have augmented it, especially since this was all against a backdrop of Charmaine and her sister Anne Marie being in and out of foster care every few months, with the knowledge of the West Midlands social services.

The West children came into contact with the authorities across many different institutions, and yet no social workers, teachers or hospital staff took meaningful steps and followed up.

There are certainly many out there who harbour regrets for not noticing or speaking out. Graham Letts, one of Rose's younger brothers, would later say, 'I take a lot of the blame myself, and my whole family does, but not all of it. Surely there was someone out there, social, welfare, school teachers, no end of people who could or should have done something?'

These early signs of the shocking treatment of Charmaine and Anne Marie had also come on the back of suspicions that Fred had killed a young boy with his ice-cream van in Glasgow in the mid-sixties. Already there were allegations of Fred using the ice cream work as a cover for preying on young victims, but no real investigation happened after the young boy was killed.

***

In the late 1960s, Terry Crick, a fellow resident at the caravan park where Fred lived, had reported him to the police. Fred had shown him a collection of what Crick called 'numerous dirty implements' that he was using to perform 'backstreet abortions'. Crick was disturbed by this, and so he set off for the local police station. This was not the first time Fred had been linked to an abortion – as early as 1962, Fred had conducted an abortion on Rena that was allegedly reported to the police but came to nothing.

The police did not act on Crick's tip-off, and theories abound as to why this was the case.

Janet Bates, Crick's wife, would later claim to the press that the police failed to act because West was a valuable police informant to them. Another national newspaper would go on to make the explosive claim that six police officers regularly paid for sex at 25 Cromwell Street and must have known at least some of what was happening behind the closed doors of this family home.

Alison Chambers, the final victim killed in Cromwell Street, had a friend who laid a complaint that Fred had raped her and that the act was witnessed by a police officer who had actively encouraged Fred to do it.

On occasion, the police would indeed come knocking on the door of what became the infamous address, but the raids carried out – whether real or staged – hinged on the hunt for illegal drugs on the premises. They would stride through the door, rifle around a little, book one or two of the lodgers for a minor marijuana indiscretion, and then walk away. The dark irony in prosecuting the residents of 25 Cromwell Street for a few grams of marijuana while unspeakable horrors were unfolding right under their noses at the same time is chilling.

It would later also be noted in a review of one of the many television documentaries that came out that one officer recalled his mother having been a lodger at the Cromwell Street house. This could have been a coincidence but appears odd in light of the fact that petty crime and prostitution were taking place under that same roof. It begs the questions: how would Rose and Fred not be afraid of having a policeman's mother living in the semi, and likewise, why would a policeman's mother choose to reside at a house that had seen its fair share of petty crimes? These allegations add substance to the as yet unproven theory that Fred was an informer.

Barely two years after Terry Crick had reported Fred to the authorities, the case of Caroline Owens came before the court. After a brutal night of sexual violence, she was brave enough to go to the police and lay a charge against the couple. But no police officers would make the connection between Caroline's accusation and the dark story shared by Crick, who was said to be so consumed by guilt and anger over his inability to stop the Wests that he committed suicide many years later when the crimes came to light.

When the Wests received a slap on the wrist in the form of a paltry £50 fine each after Caroline Owens's case, and the police decided it was 'in their best interests' for him to be kept out of prison, the nightmare had only just begun. This fatal misstep was about to cost many other young women and girls their lives, starting with little Charmaine who was only eight.

The police force has a lot to answer for in this case. But what about the education system and the responsibility of the teachers to their students? What did they think about the children who so often arrived at school covered in bruises and welts? Heather, Mae, Anne Marie and Stephen all attended Hucclecote Secondary School in Gloucester, but nobody in authority there spotted similar injuries on the children. In 1988, Fred admitted to one of Stephen's teachers that he had 'laid the boy out', but the teacher failed to report that up the chain.

There is a record of Anne Marie's teacher reporting that the child was covered in bruises in 1973, and a social worker did go around to look in on her, but nothing ever came of that either. Years later, one of Anne Marie's school reports showed that she was absent for 68 school days in one year and made reference to her mood swings. But just as nobody from the halls of education had ever checked up on Charmaine for no longer appearing in class, so nobody saw fit to question Anne Marie's dire absenteeism.

Heather did once confide in a school friend, Marie Gardner, and admitted her injuries were inflicted by her mother, who had beaten her and told her she was 'a little bitch'. That same friend would later describe how a physical education teacher had once questioned Heather about the bruises that were clearly from hands gripping her body.

Marie had told her parents about Heather's plight at home, but her father was a friend of Fred's, so it wasn't long before he told Fred what he'd been told. That gained Heather nothing but an additional beating with more punishments and restrictions. Certainly, Fred was worried enough about the banter that he began to walk Heather to and from school to prevent her from chatting idly to any of her mates.

Mae's experience at school was remarkably similar to that of her big sisters. She undressed for physical education in private, never took part in any extracurricular activities and her parents never attended a single school function. She chose not to have any friends come around to the house after she brought a boyfriend home one day and her mother walked into the room stark naked.

***

If the crimes were hidden from the police and the bruising hidden from teachers, the one group who could not claim they knew nothing about the injuries were the doctors and nurses at the various hospitals around the city. Between the years 1972 and 1992, various West family members were treated over 31 times for conditions like thrush, gonorrhoea, an 'accident' with a sledgehammer and a whole catalogue of injuries to tendons, fingers and chests, as well as lacerations between the toes of the children, some supposedly self-inflicted.

A vaginal injury sustained by Anne Marie in 1971 and treated at the Gloucester Royal Hospital was described as an injury from a chopper bike by the West parents to the hospital staff. And when that same girl arrived as a fifteen-year-old, covered in bruises and pregnant, how did nobody put two and two together? The report's sole observation is that 'an interview with her father gave the impression of being a caring and attentive parent concerned for his daughter's well-being'.

The art of portraying themselves as a normal functional family had been perfected by Rose and Fred over the years, and they also knew that the hospitals would be unlikely to share records.

But even so, how many of these visits to the hospital resulted in a case being referred to social services? Not even one.

The shameful truth is that the very first time the West children were officially identified as victims of abuse was only in 1992.

In its scathing article about the failure to stop the Wests, the *Independent* summed it all up by saying that 'by the late 1980s, each public body in Gloucester had lengthy records on the Wests, from school and hospital files to Frederick West's criminal records, which showed 10 court appearances and a prison sentence. There was, in addition, the rape of 17-year-old Caroline Owens in 1972, for which the Wests, charged with indecent assault, were fined 50 pounds each'. Over the years, there were at least four other instances when young women claimed that a man matching Fred West's description had tried to abduct them, but nothing ever came of these reports.

So many of the victims slipped through the cracks of a system because it was unable to make connections, and for their part, Rose and Fred had presented themselves as unremarkable members of a banal street in Gloucester.

If their talent for hiding the truth lay beyond their decades-long reign of terror, then so did luck. Year after year, victim after victim, things went in their favour. Until eventually, with the disappearance of Heather, the whole facade would come crashing down.

11

End Of The Line

Sometime in the early nineties, Fred West, who had always been a hustler telling tall stories about his abilities in order to get work, opened the door of his car and strode towards the office of a man named Derek Thompson.

Derek owned a construction company, and Fred, who had answered an ad in the local papers, had brought the whole family with him on a Sunday morning. When Derek caught a glimpse of Rose, he was a bit perplexed by the image she portrayed. There she was, a woman of almost forty, with her hair in two little pigtails like a schoolgirl and a pair of white ankle socks to go with the look. Also in the car were some of the Wests' many children.

Derek saw before him a man who was prepared to work hard, and over the next two years, he was proven right. His employee was no brilliant craftsman, but a hard worker he most certainly was. Derek discovered that, unlike some of his other workers who preferred to be with their families on public holidays, Fred would jump at the chance to work even on Christmas or New Year's Day. And so, with such a reliable worker at hand, Derek would phone him up whenever needed, whether day or night.

But Fred had one habit that would annoy Derek and his wife, Wendy: he would jabber in the car on the way to every job. He would just talk and talk, spewing outlandish stories about properties he owned, accidents he had just narrowly avoided, and the like. Neither Derek nor Wendy took this 'nonsense' seriously and simply let Fred spin his fantastical yarns, letting them 'go in one ear and out the other', as they would say later in an interview.

Among these tall stories were ones about big orgies in which he was taking part, but even those did not ruffle the feathers of the Thompsons, who were simply relying on Fred to help on construction sites.

It was during that period that the Wests' daughter Louise hit puberty, and she became Fred's next incestuous rape victim. Logic would suggest that Fred was also raping Tara, who was a year older than Louise, but in fact he wasn't, and the reason behind this is as disturbing as it was 'lucky' for Tara.

She would later say in an interview that Louise was raped and she wasn't because Louise was his 'natural daughter' and thus treated as 'his property', whereas she (Tara) was left alone because she had a different biological father.

On one specific day in 1992, Fred called out Louise's name. He was yelling for her to bring some bottles to a room on the first floor of the family home. Louise did as she was told, and her siblings saw her leave the room and make her way up the stairs.

Within minutes, Louise's siblings heard her crying out in pain, 'No, don't!' and a few minutes after that, the stairs creaked as their father came down to the ground floor wearing a casual face as if it were just a normal day or moment.

But when the siblings went to check up on their sister who had been crying out, they found her in a shocking state. She was in severe pain, writhing around on the bed and sobbing her eyes out. She now told her siblings the awful truth: Fred had brutally raped her, both vaginally and anally, and had also partially strangled her.

Louise was in physical and psychological agony, and she was desperate for Rose to get home so she could tell her what her father had done. But as Rose stepped through the door of the house and was taken into Louise's confidence, she responded to the story of the brutal rape by saying, 'You were asking for it.'

Very quickly, these attacks became more regular, and on one occasion, even worse than telling her daughter she had 'asked for it', Rose actually stationed herself in the same room and watched the attack take place. When Fred had satisfied his twisted desires, climbed off and left the room, Louise was in severe pain all over again and was bleeding. This time, her mother even followed her into the bathroom and asked, 'Well, what did you expect?'

Then, in another shocking act of depravity, Fred took it one step further and actually filmed himself raping Louise.

The mental and physical abuse of the West children at the hands of their own parents had always made them afraid to speak out. It had also given them the toxic confusion that children from violent homes often experience: they are biologically primed to have an innate desire to bond with their caregivers (who are most commonly their biological parents) at all costs – even if those 'costs' include living with extreme abuse.

But a few weeks later, Louise broke the mould of the West children being silenced by their own fear and confusion. Sitting alone with a school friend, and only thirteen years of age, she found the strength within herself to tell her friend what her father had been doing to her. Despite being brainwashed by her parents that all fathers broke their daughters' virginity as an act of preparation, Louise mustered the courage to tell the truth.

And in that moment, a whole chain of events would begin.

Her friend thought it best to tell an adult, and she repeated the horrific stories that Louise had told her to her mother. That was on 4 August 1992.

The mother, for her part, felt the police should be informed of these horrific claims and made an anonymous phone call to the local station.

Some 48 hours later, on the warm, late summer Thursday of 6 August, Derek Thompson was sitting at his desk at work when the phone rang – the same clunky telephone he had always used to get hold of Fred West when he needed him for some construction work.

The voice on the other end of the line announced, 'This is the police. We're calling you in connection with your employee, Fred West.'

Derek, who had only known Fred as a hard worker with a real blabbermouth and inflated ego, was about to become the lynchpin in his downfall. The police asked him to take part in a sting operation by pretending he had work for him and that he should come over to the office straight away.

Fred, of course, obliged, imagining that later that week he could add this job to the meticulous timesheets he kept to claim his pay from the Thompsons. He packed up his tools and headed over, his head no doubt filled with all the tall stories he planned to share with Derek en route to the job.

But when he got there, the police were waiting for him.

Now, one would imagine this striking terror in the heart of a person who had committed such heinous crimes. But not Fred West. As the police escorted him away, he seemed unfazed and told Derek, 'Don't worry, I'll be back soon.'

Far from being transported to the house where a search was about to take place, Fred had been caught in the sting operation for the exact opposite reason. The police wanted him out of the house so they could carry out their search as they saw fit without the main suspect interfering and being a hindrance to what needed to happen.

Over at Cromwell Street, Rosemary West, who had said goodbye to her husband and seen the children off to school, was at home when she heard a knock at the door at around 9 a.m. Perhaps she thought it was a client who had come for some early Thursday morning fun, but instead, it was a clutch of detectives.

Bear in mind that at this point, murder was not even on the cards. It was purely to do with Louise's case, and the police held in their hands a search warrant. They said they were there to search for stolen property, but their real aim was to rifle around for evidence of pornography and child abuse.

Rose West responded in the way that only Rose West would. She flew into a blind rage, screaming profanities at the uniformed officials in front of her and even physically attacking one of the policewomen.

She was immediately placed under arrest for obstruction of justice, with the police then combing the house for evidence as planned.

Trawling through the paraphernalia, they were able to procure almost a hundred videos that were pornographic in nature. Some of these had been commercially made, but some were amateur home videos of the many sexual fetishes that had been played out at 25 Cromwell Street.

Unfortunately, however, the police did not find a tape depicting Louise, which would have been all they needed to secure an airtight conviction. Instead, at the young age of thirteen, she had to find the courage to make a full statement detailing the sexual violence and abuse committed by her father. To this end, a specially trained solicitor was brought in, someone who could get such a young person to feel safe enough to tell their story.

One of the most shocking facts to be shared that day was that Fred had actually first raped her when she was only eleven years old. She also detailed in this session how she had turned to her mother for solace or protection but had received quite the opposite in return.

With the police having been taken behind the door of at least some of the dark secrets of 25 Cromwell Street, they could now act swiftly. They boxed and removed a number of items, but more importantly, the five youngest West children still living at the house were escorted outside in a joint operation between police and social services and whisked off in a state-owned car. They were taken ten miles away beyond the bustling streets of the city to the historic Cowley Manor with its palatial proportions and rolling green gardens. This was owing to the Emergency Protection Orders that had been invoked.

At the time, the manor had been in the possession of the Gloucestershire County Council for four decades and was being used as a conference centre. And so, for the first time ever, the youngest batch of West children found themselves in an entirely strange context, suddenly plucked from their home where horrors had been normalised.

It was only now, after so many missed moments, that the police went into first gear to try to uncover what had been taking place at this banal-looking little semi in an ordinary street in Gloucester. They went about interviewing the children at some length, with one of the interviews lasting as long as one and a half days.

And it was only now in the care of the state, tucked away behind the closed doors of a medical facility waiting for the doctors and social workers to arrive, that these children began to speak. And when they did, they revealed at least some of the history of their lives at 25 Cromwell Street. It was mapped all over their bodies: bruises, welts, scars – countless signs of only a fraction of what Rosemary and Fred West had inflicted on their children and got away with. The doctors were also able to clearly see the signs of sexual abuse and violations, and this was the first time in their lives that the horrific secrets of their family household were, to some degree, laid bare.

At first, the West children were terrified of using their own voices against their parents, but eventually, emboldened enough to tell at least some of the truth, they revealed that the lines were blurred but that their mother had been the primary inflictor of the physical abuse and their father the sexual.

It was also during one of these early interviews that a West child first alluded, in an off-handed manner, to the idea of Heather being buried under the patio. It was neither officially recorded nor followed up on, and it was simply seen as an absurd 'inside joke' in the family.

Besides which, at this particular point, the ill-treatment of the children was the priority of the day, and Heather was only considered as another potential witness to corroborate the stories the five children were sharing.

But with more than enough evidence in the bag from the children who were present, the state charged Fred with three counts of rape and one of sodomy. Rose, for her part, was charged with being an accomplice, with child cruelty and with inciting her husband to rape their daughter.

But still, the biggest missing piece of this puzzle from the family at 25 Cromwell Street was the eldest daughter, Heather, who had mysteriously vanished five years prior with a veil of silence – or rather, vague stories that never looked the same – drawn over her absence.

Fred insisted Heather was alive and living happily and independently of her family, that she was supporting herself by selling sex just as her mother had done. Rose wore that blank face she had always perfected between her violent rages and said she had no clue at all where Heather could be or why she had closed the door of 25 Cromwell Street behind her, never to return, one morning when her siblings were at school.

Then she changed her tune. Suddenly, she claimed she did in fact know Heather's fate, and what had happened was that she, Rose, had pulled Heather aside and advised her to leave the home lest she be a bad influence 'as a lesbian' on her younger siblings. She embellished the story a little further and said she had pushed £600 into the teenager's hands to incentivise her to depart the family lodging. Rose also claimed that, from time to time, the phone would ring and Heather's voice would come through for a little chat, and that this was proof she was not missing.

***

Fred West sat in his cell, held on remand in a Birmingham jail, as he awaited trial. The short man with dark hair like a scouring brush and pale blue eyes would still not budge. As far as he was concerned, he had done 'nothing wrong'.

Upon hearing this bald-faced lie, his eldest daughter, Anne Marie, contacted the police to share a story, one which stood in very sharp contrast to her father's claims of innocence. And she did not hold back. In fine brush strokes, she painted a word picture of all the horrific experiences that had befallen her as a child growing up in the cruel hands of her stepmother and father. She also signed on the dotted line, confirming she would be willing to testify against them when the case came to trial.

For her husband Chris Davis, it probably felt like a lifetime had passed since he sat with his wife's beautiful young sister Heather, with her dark sad eyes and liquorice-coloured hair, and advised her on how to avoid eating poisonous berries should she ever get her wish to live alone in the Forest of Dean. In reality, it had been five years, and she was nowhere to be seen.

Now, he was looking into the eyes of a police official who asked him to share details about Heather and her siblings' lives. He told them how deeply unhappy Heather had been. He said that she had never spelled it out that her father was brutally raping her but had given him enough cause for concern that he offered to take it up with them on her behalf. But young Heather had asked her brother-in-law not to do this and said that her parents would 'kill [them] both' if he went that route.

He now suggested to police that they do everything in their power to track Heather down so that she could corroborate the stories of rape and violence of which Anne Marie, his wife, had spoken.

Anne Marie, in giving a detailed account of her life under the roof of Fred and Rosemary, had also put it on record that her mother Rena and half-sister Charmaine had also lost contact with her when she was little and that she found this very strange. Attempts to contact them, as had been the case with her sister Heather, had proven futile.

By the time the authorities had sat down with Mae to draw a statement from her too, she had caught wind of Louise's change of heart. Her little sister, clearly still caught in the web of confusion brought on by the manipulation of her parents, had been afraid to continue with the case. The hard-won bravery of following through after confiding in a school friend who had told her mother was now melting under the heat of having to follow through with getting her dad imprisoned. And Mae, saddened by her little sister's confusion, took her cues from her and denied the horrors she had endured in the cellar of the house.

It would now come down to Heather and the urgency of locating her so that she could corroborate or deny Anne Marie's descriptions of rape and violence in the homestead. Detective Constable Hazel Savage was determined to track her down, so important was her testimony. But every lead took her to a dead end, even an inquiry at Inland Revenue and the Social Security Department, who found no trace of Heather ever having sought employment or drawn state benefits.

Two months would pass before officials from social services in Gloucester would contact the police and detail how perplexed they were that Heather was, quite simply, nowhere to be found.

This was to have two important consequences: on the one hand, it meant Anne Marie's story was now floating without an anchor to secure it down, and on the other hand, it inflamed the suspicions of Detective Constable Hazel Savage, who would not accept the story that Heather had left to build a life for herself elsewhere.

And so, on 7 June 1993, ten months after Savage and her team had combed through the family home and left with pornographic evidence and ordered the children be removed from the home, the case collapsed. By then, Louise had decided not to testify, and Anne Marie, a key witness, followed suit, having seen how the impending trial was taking its toll on the mental health of her younger siblings and now claiming it was all just a 'figment of her imagination'. She was also, after all these years, still terrified of her volatile stepmother who had beaten her body and terrorised her mind.

With an acquittal safely in hand, Rose and Fred hugged one another in the dock and got off scot-free.

This was an eerie replay of what had happened some thirty years prior, when Fred's own sister Kitty had lost her nerve at the last minute and declined to press charges against her brother who was raping her.

12

Where Is Heather?

With the trial against them having collapsed, and their children's ingrained fear of them having worked in their favour, Rose and Fred West – officially acquitted – made their way back to 25 Cromwell Street, where they opened the door onto the house where so much had already happened and where secrets oozed from every inch.

It was much quieter now, the sounds of the children having departed with their sudden removal almost a year before. Sure, they would still visit on occasion, but it was always under the beady eye of an official from social services. The children's days at Cowley Manor had turned into weeks and weeks into months.

By then, members of the extended family had by and large cut ties with them, but those who clung to the last threads of belief that Rose and Fred were just a sweet married couple were told the same story: that the police had a vendetta against them and had fabricated the whole sorry story.

But in a small office littered with papers over at the police station, Detective Constable Hazel Savage was still not satisfied. Perhaps Anne Marie's insistence was contagious – her insistence that the disappearance of her mother and two half-siblings was still beyond logic. Or perhaps the constable simply had a hunch that wouldn't go away. Or perhaps, most likely, the forensic evidence before her was a clear case of a deeper dig being needed. Three people from the same family cannot simply vanish into thin air and become untraceable in a country that has unemployment benefits, social security numbers, police records …

Over the next few months, the West children were intermittently interviewed by the authorities, but, well trained by brutality over the years, they still let little slip about the scale of horror experienced in their daily lives.

Then, one day, one of the children made a throwaway remark about 'Heather being under the patio', before dismissing it as the family joke. The attending social worker didn't think much of the comment at first. After all, this was not a criminal investigation or a missing persons case. This was about child protection.

Anne Marie, who was of course much older and not living in state care at Cowley Manor, was also asked about the 'family joke' of Heather being buried beneath the patio. As she had already moved out by the time Heather disappeared from their lives, she had not been among the small children for whom their sister's alleged burial 'under the patio' could be used as a jocular mantra to strike fear in their hearts. She then said she had indeed heard Fred utter these words, but only once and not in any meaningful way. He had then burst out laughing, and she had bought into not taking the statement seriously.

But over the months, as Rose and Fred's vice-like hold on their children's psyches began to loosen, the children began to open up. Now and then, the children would, at different times, reference the family 'joke' that Heather was buried under the patio. It was, however, being told to different officials at different times by different children, and nobody held the thread to pull it all together. The comments were also made in the same offhand manner, and it is unlikely the children believed their sister was buried there. It is more likely they were repeating the 'joke' their parents often made.

But by August 1993, there was enough concern among the social workers to examine things in more detail. The police were alerted, and as they looked more closely into Heather's disappearance, they became increasingly perplexed at the absence of any records suggesting she was still alive.

The police had also, in the interim, mapped out Fred's history, which included the existence and then disappearance of his stepchild Charmaine and her mother Rena. But what they found most confusing was that no missing person report had ever been opened and yet no signs of their existence elsewhere came to the fore.

Still, the officers hardly rushed over to investigate. They pledged to intensify their search for Heather West, but with their heavy caseloads, it wasn't a major priority, and once again, beautiful young Heather and her disappearance were not given the attention it deserved. She remained unaccounted for, and another year would pass without her showing up.

At the same time, Anne Marie would still not let go of a story that haunted and confused her in equal measure: Charmaine, with whom she shared a mother, and Heather, with whom she shared a father, had seemingly vanished into thin air. And Rena, her and Charmaine's mother, had had the same fate. Anne Marie could not accept it, and though she had not testified against her father in the case of sexual abuse, she definitely wasn't going to let this go.

Years later, Anne Marie would describe the retraumatisation of sharing the story of Heather's disappearance with Constable Savage. She said it brought back horrors she thought she had blocked out forever, and that it shook her to her core with trauma to describe it all over again.

And finally, the police set down some tables and chairs and invited all the social workers who'd been involved with the West children. Here, they would ask the right questions and record the responses so that dots could finally be joined. What had been quoted as a family joke had become a piece of forensic evidence that had the potential to reveal an almost unimaginable scenario − that a couple had murdered their own child in cold blood, buried her under the patio at the family home where they still lived, and then joked about this as a way of scaring their surviving children into behaving.

All the social workers' words were collected into a dossier of evidence, and finally, a search warrant under Section 8 of the Police and Criminal Evidence Act of 1984 was granted.

An official in the Gloucestershire Police crunched all this information down into the cold words of the law, and typed up a statement: 'Having exhausted all enquiries to trace Heather, it was decided that formal witness statements should be obtained from social workers closely connected with the West children relating to the "family joke." With the evidence contained in those statements, together with the result of other police enquiries, successful application was made to Gloucester Magistrates for a search warrant under Section 8 of the Police and Criminal Evidence Act 1984 enabling the police to search 25 Cromwell Street for evidence relating to Heather's whereabouts.'

It was 23 February 1994 when the Gloucester police had successfully obtained their warrant and made their way over to the house in Cromwell Street. With Detective Inspector Tony James at the helm, fifteen officers arrived and stood in front of the same door that so many lodgers, clients, victims and children had knocked at.

It was 1.25 p.m., and when Rosemary West opened the door to see the band of officers before her and was handed a copy of the search warrant, she turned white as a ghost and flew into a rage.

She screamed over her shoulder to her son Stephen, who by then was a grown man of 21, 'Get Fred!'

She ran back inside to call Fred but discovered he was on a job with Derek and his mobile phone was not working. She then called on Derek's phone and asked him to please locate her husband so she could speak to him.

Derek would later describe hearing Rose screaming hysterically on the other end of the phone, telling Fred that the police had arrived at their house and wanted to dig up the garden.

And Fred, the man who had never kept his mouth shut for a single moment with all the tall stories tumbling out to 'impress' the Thompsons, was now as quiet as a mouse. He stood rooted to the ground trying to make out his wife's hysterical words, and then handed the phone back to Derek.

He left the construction site without saying a single other word, and that was the very last time Derek Thompson ever clapped eyes on him. It was 1.40 p.m., a time at which Fred West would normally have wolfed down a sandwich before carrying on with his work, but on this particular day, his world was about to crumble.

Over at 25 Cromwell Street, they calculated that Fred would arrive home within the next half an hour, as that is how long it takes to do the ten miles from Stroud, where he was working that day, back to Gloucester.

But half an hour turned into an hour, and then the entire afternoon slipped away with the house now shrouded in an air of horrible potential outcomes.

Detective Sergeant Terry Onions was the first police officer who now had the opportunity to interview Rose West. No longer shielded by her wily husband, who would only arrive home much later, she now had no choice but to answer some questions.

Stretching all the way back to the days of tying little Charmaine to a chair and beating her and sexually abusing her sister Anne Marie, Rose had committed one crime after another. She had raped, beaten, murdered, tortured, physically assaulted and psychologically abused so many young women and children. Over more than two decades, the law had not caught up with her. Now, cornered by the authorities in her own home, she became defiant and defensive. The recorded interviews from that day in 1994 offer a rare glimpse into the mind of a woman who treated human beings as instruments for her own twisted pleasure.

She couldn't have known that her freedom would soon be ripped away, but she was getting her first taste of what accountability looks like when you've got blood on your hands.

While they waited for Fred to return, Onions began his interview by going straight to the possible whereabouts of Heather.

'We have come here to talk to you about your daughter Heather. We are concerned about her, where she might be. As we interview you about your daughter's disappearance, I had better caution you, which means you are not obliged to say anything. What is she in the family line?' began Onions.

Rose said Heather was her firstborn and came into the world on 17 October 1970. She said that Heather had left a long time ago when she was around age seventeen. Onions asked when she last saw her, and from that moment, Rose began building lie upon lie, however implausible.

> Terry Onions (TO): We are talking seven years ago … about 1987. Do you remember what month it was? Spring? Summer?

Rosemary West (RW): I can't remember.
TO: What were the causes of her going, then?
RW: Lots of things really. Mainly I suppose because she was unhappy.
TO: What was the reason ... she wasn't happy ...
RW: I don't know. We had problems with her at school, things like that.
TO: Was she in school?
RW: She was nearly 17 so she had left school.
TO: Could she have left at Christmas or did she carry on until the summer?
RW: I would say it was the summer.

Rose presented as the opposite of a bereft mother who had not seen or heard from her child for seven years. Likewise, she bore none of the traits of a nervous suspect, layering over lies with anxiety or dramatic denials. Instead, from the very first word of the exchange, she appeared evasive and non-committal. It was as if none of this really mattered and the detective was simply a bothersome guest.

After a few minutes, the detectives shifted their focus to the day of Heather's disappearance.

TO: Was there any row before she left?
RW: I suppose there must have been raised voices. I don't know, I was upset. She said she didn't want to stay.
TO: You tried to persuade her to stay, did you?
RW: I said 'What are you going to do?' I had a problem with her because I knew what she was. That was what made it tricky with the other children. She was a lesbian, as far as I know.
TO: She was a very young girl. How did you know that? You had a picture in your mind of what a lesbian was like and she fitted it?

RW: That's right. One particular incident, her uncle was talking to her. He said to her about boyfriends or something and he said, 'You know, you had better watch it like, because they get up to tricky things.' She said, 'If any boy put his hand on my knee I'd put a f***ing brick over his head.'

TO: That doesn't particularly mean she was a lesbian. What made you think she was definitely a lesbian?

RW: In the infants' school, she knew exactly what kind of knickers the woman teacher had on.

TO: It sounds as if you are annoyed.

RW: The only reason it annoys me is because I believe to cut off communication between me and her. Teenagers disagree with their parents. I know Mae is very close to her father.

TO: The night before there were raised voices and it was about that, was it? 'You are a lesbian'?

RW: I couldn't talk to her. There was no communication. She said she would talk to her father. That was it. You can lead a horse to water but you can't make it bloody drink. She was a stubborn girl – you ask the rest of the family. She didn't want to do her own washing. From what was going around at school, so I can gather, she had obviously had it planned for some time. I left her to talk to her father and went and did some shopping.

As the interview progressed, Rose became more talkative and indignant. Her disdain for Heather could not be disguised, and she began to list all her daughter's traits that irritated her and the many things she had, in Rose's eyes, done wrong.

Rose also told the police that she had given Heather some money on the days before she left. Realising that money amounts to something traceable, she tried to backtrack.

TO: As regards the bank account, we would like to find out if there's some fact in your story. £600 is a lot of money. If it was me, considering that was a really stressful time for me, my first one moving away, and then I went to the bank to make sure she had some money, I would know which bank ...

RW: I was upset at the time. I was upset ... what do you think? I'm a f***ing computer? In the last 18 months, I have had f***ing hell. What more do you want?

TO: I'm trying to find out if Heather is still alive.

RW: If you had any brains at all, you could find her. It can't be that difficult.

TO: We could actually pinpoint the day she went – from your account. What did she take with her?

RW: I don't know. I wasn't there.

TO: Did you go and look in her bedroom?

RW: Yes.

TO: Have you seen her since?

RW: No.

TO: Have you heard from her since?

RW: No. She obviously doesn't want us any more, does she?

TO: How did she get from here?

RW: I don't know.

TO: Did you go and ask her school friends? Did you ask them why she had gone?

RW: No.

TO: What inquiries have you made?

RW: When you have brought up a girl like that and you have done everything and then they turn round and turn their back on you, that's it. She didn't want to know me.

TO: Teenage and parent trouble is our business. It's a part in everybody's life.

RW: All I put it down to is that I don't agree with what she is doing. That's obvious. She has always been an obstinate child. She didn't want to do anything that anybody else was doing. She left school and she just sat in the chair.
TO: Did she give you any idea where she was going?
RW: No.

Rose had come across as a sulky teenager: resentful of the questions, giving monosyllabic answers and brushing off any deeper questioning with clear irritability.

Then the detectives went straight to the heart of the matter – the grim possibility that Heather was actually dead and buried in the garden of her own house:

TO: The reason why we have come round here is because there have been extensive inquiries since the inquiry two years ago, and from that inquiry came Heather – nobody knew where she was, or whatever. Since then, checks have been done – marriages, deaths, nationwide. Her national insurance number stops with you from birth to death. They are not all-consuming and she could have gone away and changed her identity completely. Possibly. But she wasn't particularly streetwise. She hasn't contacted – to our knowledge – another living person. Tomorrow there will be a lot of officers out there, digging that garden. If you can point us in any direction as to where she could be. Even if you can say she is anywhere in the world, it would be cheaper than having the inquiry going on. If you know where she is, I beg of you to tell us. Have you any idea where she is?
RW: No. [...]
TO: How did you used to punish her when she was naughty?

RW: I just sent her to bed.
TO: Did Fred hit her?
RW: No.
TO: What about being hit with household implements?
RW: Oh, we're back to this one. Look, just drop that one. That ain't going nowhere. I've had all those charges put on me and they were dropped.
TO: I don't know anything about that. What about the rumours of where she is? What rumours have you heard about where she is? Can you tell us?
RW: She wouldn't tell me, would she?
TO: Have you heard the children saying she is under the patio?
RW: Anna said something …
TO: Who's Anna?
RW: The big girl. She said that.
TO: The whole patio will be dug up – the garden and everything. If she is under there …
RW: There's nothing you will stop at, is there?
TO: I'm a bit of a sceptic. I've been in the job 19 years. One of the hazards of the job is that people tend to lie to us. So you will have to forgive me for being a sceptic.
RW: You are going to have to excuse me for being a sceptic as well. You think I would just turn my back and forget that I have those kids?
TO: What we are talking about now is Heather. If you know she is underneath the patio or the floor or whatever …
RW: Look, the house is yours. Have it. Do what you are going to do.
TO: So where did Anna get the feeling that Heather is under the patio from, hey?
RW: Go and ask her. I haven't spoken to her for years.
TO: Why haven't you spoken to her?

RW: Because she gave us a load of hassle when she grew up. There's no stopping them. They just go and do what they like. All you get afterwards is this sort of crap.
TO: You resent the fact that your children grew up? A lot of people say that the best time of their lives is when their children are small.
RW: I kept them clean and fit and took them to school. They never wanted for nothing.

Rose's inability to see her children as human beings with feelings, needs and agency over their own lives became increasingly apparent during this exchange. She came across as a mother who believed her children should never do anything of their own free will, and the dark subtext was that she saw them as her playthings who should always have remained as such. She was implying, also, that they should be grateful to her for the life that she and Fred had provided. Onions then asked her flat out if she believed Heather was alive.

RW: Well, why not? Unless something horrible has happened to her. Come on – hundreds of thousands of kids go missing.
TO: Heather has disappeared for some seven years without a telephone call, without contacting any person whom she had known, without any activity as regards marriage, employment …
RW: There must be something somewhere. You have just missed it, that's all.

This was the last meaningful exchange during Rose's interview at home that day. She was in a highly defensive and emotionally detached state, frequently claiming not to remember important details and giving vague or evasive answers, particularly about dates and specifics surrounding Heather leaving home.

Her responses tinged with anger and frustration, she showed no concern for her 'missing' daughter. She focused instead on all that she had found difficult, and in that moment, Rose had done little to appease the police.

She had, in fact, done just the opposite.

By 5.30 p.m., when the police officers had to head off and the sun had just set, Fred had still not arrived back at his home. It is hard to imagine where he went or what he might have done during those four hours caught in limbo between his life as a brutal rapist and murderer and the law finally having caught up with him.

One also wonders if Rose grasped the full extent of what was about to happen or if, in her usual manner, she foregrounded her rage at the expense of any deeper thought.

The officers finally left, and another two hours would pass before anyone heard from Fred.

But then, at 7.40 p.m., he darkened the doorway down at the police station, strolling inside after being absent and out of contact for six hours as if he didn't have a care in the world.

There to meet him was Detective Constable Hazel Savage, who had never given up on the idea that the absent family members could be dead, or the idea that Heather being buried under the house was not so absurd as to be impossible.

Still a free man, Fred now sat down on a chair opposite the detective and listened to what she had to say.

Then he began speaking, but far from finally coming clean since the law had caught up with him, instead he declared 'there must be some mistake'. He kept his cold blue eyes as still as possible with no hint of panic and told the detective that he had last seen Heather in Birmingham.

Technically speaking, at this point there were no formal charges against him, no confession and no actual evidence.

Perhaps he was confident he had got away with his monstrous activities once or possibly he knew in his heart that this was the end of the road, but either way, he strode out of the police station and finally made his way home.

Mae and Stephen, two grown-ups staying temporarily at their abusive childhood home once more to provide emotional support to their mother, now watched as she stood at the kitchen window, whispering to Fred about what the police had been asking them and glancing intermittently towards the excavation site in the back garden.

Less than an hour later, Rose stepped out of the house with Fred and the dogs in tow. It was pitch dark and the middle of winter, and they likely cut two very lonely figures as they headed down to Gloucester Park.

There they walked, the condensation of each one's breath visible in the air as they spoke in hushed tones with the dogs trailing behind them. After a short while, they headed back home, and for the last time ever, Rosemary West climbed into bed beside her husband Fred, the man she had met at fifteen, a quarter of a century before. And as they switched off the lights, they both had an unusual feeling: they could sense they were nearing a turn in the road with no idea where it would lead.

13

The Confession

When the sun rose over Gloucester on Friday 25 February 1994, an exhausted police officer breathed a sigh of relief. His night vigil over a house earmarked for excavation the next day was over. He had been stationed there since the previous evening to make sure Rosemary and Fred West did not flee from their home or tamper with the digging that had slowly begun. Now he could leave and return home to claim his sleep in a warm bed.

Behind the walls of the semi at 25 Cromwell Street, a home he had stood beside all evening, a serial killing tragedy that had begun in the late 1960s was about to be revealed.

And the murderous couple with blood on their hands now had nothing to do but wait for the knock at the door – the knock of a detective armed with a pen and paper.

In the early hours of that same morning, when Stephen was about to leave for work, Fred said to him, 'Look, son. Look after mum and sell the house. I've done something really bad.'

And then he added, 'I want you to go to the papers and make as much money as you can.'

After Stephen left, the morning moved along at a crawl for Rose and Fred until eventually, at quarter past eleven, a police car pulled up outside, followed by the knock on the door they had been half-expecting for much of their lives.

Fred opened the door and standing there was Detective Constable Hazel Savage, a tough woman who had never given up on the West family, even when stories were hard to pin down. It had taken more than just a slight effort to convince her senior colleagues that a search warrant was in order in the first place. But she had remained steadfast all along in her conviction that Heather's remains could well be under the patio, as so frequently referenced in the family 'joke'.

With seven years having passed since Heather's disappearance, it was this self-same constable who had ascertained that Heather's national insurance number lay dormant and that Heather, in all those seven years, had neither sought nor found work.

Now here she was in her police uniform, standing opposite Fred West, the father of the missing girl who, by then, would have been a woman of 23. Fred asked what they wanted, and they said they had come to 'enquire about the whereabouts of a relative'.

At this point, Fred led them into the living room. And sitting there, as if it were a normal school day with the children all out the house and a client about to make his way up to Mandy's room, was Rose, plonked in front of the television set watching some inane show.

When one of them spoke to her, she stared blankly in their direction, and it was clear one of her rages was boiling up inside. Fred now took action, leading Rose out of the room into the hallway.

The two of them stood there quietly speaking just for a minute or two with the door to the living room kept firmly shut, and then Fred came back into the living room with an astonishing announcement: he wanted to accompany the detectives and travel with them back to the station.

The detectives nodded and escorted him out the house and into the police vehicle in which they had arrived, with Rose keeping silent as she watched the goings-on.

She was not the only one with eyes on the scene. All the neighbours, some of whom had been there for many years and others who had moved in too recently to have met any of the lodgers, gawped at what was unfolding.

And, before Detective Law had even turned the keys in the ignition, Fred blurted out the words that would shine a light of revelation onto what Detective Savage had fought so long to prove: his daughter Heather had indeed been killed, and her remains were buried in the garden of the family home.

Referencing the short moments of shallow digging from the day before, he added, 'You've been digging in the wrong place.'

This confession was a staggering about-turn in a very short space of time. Just the day before, Fred had rubbished the claims that there was any substance to the oft-repeated phrase in the family that Heather was beneath the patio. He had even tried to belittle the officers by saying that they were just treating him badly because of their grudge against him on account of his acquittal in the case of Louise's rape.

But now, at 11.20 a.m. on the very next day, just a few minutes after the detectives had arrived, Fred West was placed under arrest for the murder of his daughter Heather. Sitting cuffed in the back of the CID police vehicle, he glanced out of the window to see the neighbours taking it all in, and not long after, he was formally charged with murdering his daughter.

An hour later, Rose heard another knock at the door. This time, there was no wiggle room to ignore the officers' questions or stare into the television set. She was arrested on the spot, handcuffed, and driven off to the Cheltenham Police Station for a second police interview.

The authorities now held a crucial trump card over Rose. She had no idea that Fred had confessed to the murder. While the first interview the day before had been fairly wide-ranging, this one was going to focus exclusively on Heather – the police needed to know how much Rose knew about her daughter's disappearance, whether she was in cahoots with Fred or whether she would be a useful witness in the case they were beginning to build.

Once again, it was Detective Sergeant Terry Onions who led the questioning.

> TO: At what stage did you know she [Heather] was leaving?
> RW: She had had a job offer in Devon somewhere.
> TO: Was it her decision to leave, initially, and how long before she left had she made the decision to leave?
> RW: Members of the family believe she had it planned for quite a while.
> TO: Who did she mention it to?
> RW: I get the gist that she was determined to go because she had had this job offer and it had fallen through and she had been crying all night because she didn't get it.
> TO: Who told you that?
> RW: I think it was Stephen.
> TO: How do you understand the physical leaving taking place?
> RW: I can't remember.
> TO: Did she go with anybody?
> RW: I can't remember.

TO: This is your own eldest child.
RW: Yes.
TO: So it was quite a traumatic event.
RW: That's right.
TO: Have you seen her since that day? Have you got any inkling where she might be?
RW: She was going down to Devon and she was going to get a job with the company, no matter how long it took her.
TO: What company was this?
RW: Don't know.
TO: Did she say at any stage who she was going away with?
RW: No, not to me. I got the idea Fred was not going to tell me anything even if I did ask. She asked him not to tell me.
TO: To the average bystander, it's a very odd scenario; to suddenly disappear and not to make any inquiries must be very disturbing.
RW: She had promised to write, which we were waiting for. That never came to light either.
TO: You have never done anything to find out where she might be?
RW: Nothing. As far as I'm concerned, she left home of her own accord.
TO: Has her dad made any inquiries?
RW: Once a child does cut you off, there's not a lot you are going to be able to do to get her back. We did that with Anne Marie. Anne Marie left home four times.

At this stage, it seems as if the police wanted to see if Rose could also be caught in a lie, saying that she had spoken to Heather recently. That would make the case against her much stronger.

But Rose was deliberately vague and would only say that it was Fred who had been in contact with their eldest.

> RW: Fred has seen her in Birmingham. He has seen her in Bristol.
> TO: You believe him?
> RW: So he says.
> TO: Do you believe him?
> RW: I've got no reason not to.
> TO: When was the last time he said he saw Heather? It was in quite unusual circumstances, I would have thought. It must be a major thing and I would be expecting him to tell her mother.
> RW: He saw her when he was in Birmingham.
> TO: Is that what you are saying? And what were the circumstances? How long ago was it?
> RW: He was on bail.
> TO: He had to go up there and stay away from the family ... when was that?
> RW: Well, I haven't seen the children for about 18 months, so it must have been about then.
> TO: So Fred saw her quite recently? What did she look like?
> RW: He told me she looked rough.
> TO: What was she actually doing? Fred said she was driving a car – do you remember him saying that? Do you remember what type of car he said she was driving?
> RW: No.
> TO: So you don't remember any of that?
> RW: No.
> TO: Why do you think you've been arrested today? For the most grave of offences. There has been a

major development this morning. Fred has confessed to murdering Heather.

RW: What? So you know where she is?

TO: He has told us where she is.

RW: So she is dead, is that right?

TO: Fred has confessed to murdering Heather.

RW: What?

TO: And that automatically implicates you.

RW: (Crying) Why does it automatically implicate me?

TO: Our suspicions are aroused that you are implicated in it.

Once Rose heard that Fred had confessed, she collapsed into tears and the interview came to an end. Was she crying for her lost daughter, or was she upset that the elaborate life of lies and crime she had built with her husband had finally been brought to a halt?

During the second interview, Rose's behaviour continued to be evasive and inconsistent, though she did try to provide more specific information about Heather's departure than in the first interview. But she remained vague on many key details, claiming memory issues and often deflecting questions by referring to what Fred had said or done. Her account of Heather's leaving seemed to shift throughout the conversation, and she maintained an emotional detachment when discussing her daughter's disappearance.

It was around 6.30 p.m. that day that Fred re-entered the police vehicle, this time doing the trip the other way around, from the police station back to the house. By now it was dark outside, and the winter air lay cold over the excavation site.

Standing in his own backyard, flanked by the detectives, Fred now indicated to them without pause where he had buried Heather in the back garden.

The next day, the detectives knew, would be a long one.

And as for Rose and Fred West, the life they had known since moving into this house in 1972 was over, and it was just a matter of hours before the address 25 Cromwell Street would become synonymous with the most depraved crimes in English history.

14

Bringing Up The Bodies

Gloucester Police Station in Bearland sits like a set of Lego pieces painted the dullest colour imaginable. It is neither attractive nor an eyesore, and it simply wears its governmental officiousness on its sleeve. It was in this rather boring-looking building with its brown exterior walls and rows of windows that an incident room was hastily set up on the fourth floor on the morning of Saturday 26 February 1994.

There, Detective Superintendent John Bennett stood in front of the maps, notebooks and photographs as he led the team that was excavating the home of Heather West as they searched for the girl's body.

At this point, it was only the fate of Heather West that the police had set their sights on, and even in that case, her slippery parents kept changing their stories.

Over the course of that Saturday morning, authorisation was given for the detention of both the West parents to be extended as the police drew closer to the truth and the digging began again in earnest back at the family home.

It was around 1.30 p.m. that day that Fred West once again did an about-turn. He now retracted without hesitation his confession that he had murdered his daughter Heather, who had not been spotted since she was sixteen years old some seven years prior. He then stuck with the retraction for the remainder of all interviews carried out that day, stating without hesitation that he had made it all up during his earlier confession and that Heather was indeed alive and well and living somewhere else.

But back at 25 Cromwell Street, something major was about to happen.

It was in the late afternoon light around 4 p.m. when a support group officer suddenly stopped and walked over to a crime scene officer and tapped him on the shoulder. The support group officer had turned rather pale, and he told his colleague that he had found a bone.

But strangely, the bone he had stumbled upon was not in the section of garden that Fred had earlier indicated was the spot where Heather was buried. The bone was extracted with painstaking care, placed in a special container, and transported back to the incident room.

There, the Home Office pathologist Professor Bernard Knight, with his stern mouth but friendly eyes, carefully took the bone and began his careful examination of what was the first bone to be found at 25 Cromwell Street.

It did not take him long to realise it was a human femur, and with that, he left the station and returned to the dig site accompanied by officers. He now began excavating the site that had been pinpointed by Fred West as the place where Heather's remains could be found.

And sure enough, a collection of bones in a decaying bin bag was soon discovered.

These turned out to be Heather's, exactly as Fred had said, but now came the shock for all those present: among Heather's bones were both her femurs, which meant that the first bone found by the supporting officer belonged to someone else.

Fred was dragged back into the interview room and his detention extended even further. On hearing the irrefutable evidence found in his garden, he changed his story back to his former claim that, indeed, he had murdered his daughter. He denied, however, that Rose had anything to do with it.

He said he had strangled his daughter in a fit of rage and then taken her lifeless body to the bathroom on the ground floor of the family home. There, he matter-of-factly recounted, he took hold of a serrated knife used for slicing frozen meat. He cut off her legs and her head, and then, placing his daughter's dismembered body in a dustbin, he rolled it down to the bottom of the garden, where he stashed it away behind the Wendy house.

When the opportunity came to bury her, it was done in a grave that he had forced Stephen to dig, pretending it was required in order to install a fish pond .

What Fred did not explain was why Heather's one kneecap and several of her fingers were missing. Neither did he explain why her fingernails were in a little pile separate from her body or why two lengths of rope were intertwined with what remained of Heather.

For Fred West, his daughter had become a puzzle of bones and flesh that were nothing more than forensic evidence.

But for Stephen, Mae and Anne Marie, the three siblings with whom she had such a strong bond, the discovery of her body was devastating, if at first incomprehensible.

When Fred's solicitor informed Stephen and Mae that their father had confessed to killing Heather, Mae went into a visible state of shock and said it wasn't true. Stephen slumped against the nearest wall and sobbed uncontrollably.

A few miles away, the landline rang at Anne Marie's house. On that day, she was hosting a birthday party for her child and had fifteen noisy kids running through the house. When she answered the phone and heard the news, she would later say in a documentary, she could literally not compute what she had just heard.

She went to the bathroom, numb and confused, and re-emerged to continue with the party. It was only later that the shock would wear off and the reality of her sister's death would make its way into her mind. That, and the truth about her other sister Charmaine and mother Rena, would take a lifetime of grief to process.

When questioned about the third femur, Fred had no choice but to admit to another murder. And it was in that very moment that what began as a search for his missing daughter was about to become something much bigger.

It was chilling for all present to discover, in one afternoon, that Heather West had indeed been murdered, that she had – exactly as per the 'family joke' – been buried beneath the patio, and that another murder had taken place.

Fred named the other victim as Shirley Robinson – though the thigh bone that had been found was actually that of Alison Chambers – and admitted that he had murdered her and buried her in the same backyard garden as his own daughter.

At 8.30 p.m. that night, the police went before the Gloucester Magistrates' Court (the same court that had told him twenty years earlier that it was not in his best interest to do any jail time) and managed to secure another 36 hours in detention for Fred West.

All the while, Fred stayed steadfast in his strategy to protect Rose. He needed the authorities to believe that just as his children had no idea about the murders, the same was true of his wife Rose.

And so it was that the last two victims of the Wests were the first two that were discovered.

This was shocking enough, but it was only the beginning of what would become one of the biggest breakthroughs in policing history. A cluster of cold cases, filed away and forgotten by all but the families, were about to be reopened, yet the horror of what would be revealed was beyond anyone's imagination.

15

One Horrific Find After Another

By the last day of February in 1993, Fred and Rosemary's reign of terror was crumbling in front of their eyes. The third femur, dug up in the garden, was proof that more than one murder had taken place, and over the next few weeks, the garden, the patio, the cellar, and sites further afield would reveal scenes of horror that had spanned more than two decades.

The names of a slate of young women and girls, whose lives had been brutally cut short, would no longer be written in faded ink, filed away under 'cold cases'. In some instances, they were cases that had never been: either nobody had ever come looking for them, or the Wests had played their old trick of claiming the person had left to live elsewhere.

But for some of the families, like the Partingtons and the Goughs, the worst nightmare of their lives was about to take a turn. The mystery of their lost loved ones would finally be solved, but the details were so gruesome that the 'not knowing' might have been easier.

On the morning of Monday 28 February, Fred had been formally charged with the murder of Heather. Two hours later, just before lunch time, he sat down on a chair at the police station and answered questions about how he had murdered Shirley Robinson, while claiming Rose knew nothing about it.

In a bizarre twist of fate, however, Shirley's bones were only discovered at 9 p.m. that evening in the back garden, several hours after he had nonchalantly described how he had murdered her. Perhaps for the monstrous Fred, all his victims had blurred into a jumble of different young women, or perhaps he couldn't quite remember where he had buried each dismembered body. Shirley had been pregnant with his child, so perhaps that is why her name came to mind first. But the bones he thought were Shirley's were actually Alison's. She was only sixteen when she was murdered, and the evidence showed that a leather belt was fastened around her head at the time of her death.

By 9 p.m., both Shirley and Alison had joined what would become a long list of those who had endured a hideous death at the hands of the Wests.

The next day, Tuesday 1 March 1994, Fred was interviewed mid-morning about the horrors he had visited upon Alison Chambers. She was the young woman who, just shy of her seventeenth birthday, had been sweet-talked with promises of life on a farm where she would be well taken care of. Being so vulnerable and living in a children's home at the time of her disappearance had worked against her both in terms of falling into the hands of the murderers and also not being properly searched for.

The most poignant detail of Alison's life and death was that it was a friendship with Anne Marie that had led her into the lair of the latter's monstrous parents. And when she had gone missing, she had been living at the house.

Her disappearance barely raised an eyebrow from the police, and here was her broken body, found fourteen years later, with the awful truth buried with her: she had been gagged, raped, tortured, dismembered and finally buried in a grave in a garden where, the killers had hoped, she would never be found.

Before her bones were removed from their secret grave in the backyard garden, Professor Bernard Knight – the same expert who had identified Heather's remains – arrived at the house to examine them.

By the end of that day, the young lives of Heather, Shirley and Alison, who still would have had so much ahead of them, had been reduced to the findings of diggers in a garden. The same could be said for Shirley's unborn baby, whose life was cut short even before birth. The bones of the victims showed the deep depravity of the West parents, and yet more were to follow.

While Heather had had the dire misfortune of being born to Fred and Rose and having endured a life of abuse before she was killed, Shirley Robinson had fallen into the dark trap of having a relationship with Fred. She was the vulnerable teenager whose fate was sealed when she stepped through the doors of the Green Lantern Cafe in 1977 looking for accommodation and shortly thereafter took up residence at 25 Cromwell Street. While Rose had at first boasted that Fred was responsible for Shirley's pregnancy, she later had become jealous and had seen Shirley as a threat.

When Shirley's body was retrieved, the forensic evidence showed that her unborn baby had been removed from her body and also had several bones missing. It is chilling to think that when Rose made her way down to the offices of Gloucester social services in an attempt to submit a false claim for maternity benefits in Shirley's name, Shirley and her unborn child were so recently buried on the property from which Rose had just departed. It is hard to imagine a more mercenary act by one mother in another mother-to-be's name.

***

With three bodies having been dug up in an ordinary semi in a banal street in Gloucester, a media frenzy gathered pace. A barrage of reporters and photographers began arriving around the clock to set up camp in Cromwell Street. Little did they know in those early days that many of them would reach out for counselling to process what they were covering on that assignment.

As the news of the dark discovery was amplified across the land, so it was that many unsolved cases began to rise up. The day after Fred's confessions about Shirley and Alison, a member of the public phoned the detectives at the police station where the incident room had been set up. Lynda Gough went missing in 1973 and she had stayed at 25 Cromwell Street, the emotional caller told the detectives. The records do not state who the caller was, but the idea of Lynda Gough's mother seeing Rose in her daughter's slippers all those years before and then seeing that same house on the news twenty years later is heartbreaking.

Still haunted by the photograph of their daughter in a checked blue dress and auburn hair hanging about her shoulders, frozen in time at age nineteen, they now faced the prospect of finally knowing the terrible truth – but only time and more digging would tell.

The next day, even as he was formally charged with the murder of Shirley and Alison, Fred West flatly denied any knowledge of Lynda Gough. It's hard to imagine what was going through his mind, but perhaps he imagined that those buried in the cellar in the house would forever remain a secret. What he also imagined, based on police records, is that Rose would be spared the punishment awaiting them as he continued to claim she was not an accomplice and it had all been him.

***

ONE HORRIFIC FIND AFTER ANOTHER

On Friday 4 March, with the teams on the ground at the house and those manning the incident room equally as exhausted and horrified, things were about to become a whole lot more gruesome. Far from believing Fred that the full extent of their serial killing had now been revealed, the police instead brought in specialist ground-scanning equipment. They wanted to know what lay behind solid matter at this house that was already proving to be a macabre trove for any investigator with unsolved cases on the books.

On the same cold Friday afternoon, Fred suddenly admitted to knowing Lynda Gough but claimed she had packed her bags and headed off to Weston-super-Mare, leaving no forwarding address or phone number in her wake. He and Rose, he claimed, had thus lost all contact with her. But when he caught wind of the scanning equipment being brought in to dig up his hideous past, he folded. By 2.30 p.m., Detective Constable Savage, who never quite let go of her deep suspicions about Fred and Rose, told him what was about to happen, that the whole house was about to be searched.

This must have been quite a moment for her, facing off with a man who now squirmed at the prospect of having his darkest secrets revealed.

Some three hours later, a handwritten note was passed to Detective Superintendent Bennett from Fred West. It read, in his uneven and spiky handwriting on a small lined piece of paper torn from a pad with small metal rings at the top: 'I, Frederick West, authorise my solicitor, Howard Ogden, to advise Superintendent Bennett that I wish to admit to a further (approx) nine killings expressly Charmaine, Rena, Lynda Gough and others to be identified.' Signed: F West.

Within the hour, he was interviewed yet again, and this time he admitted to killing and burying Lynda, Charmaine and

Rena. He also delivered, in chilling details, how he had killed Lucy Partington.

A week had passed since he had first admitted to killing Heather. And now he revealed that his home was a killing field in the middle of the urban landscape and that there were more bodies buried under the house. While Rose remained an obscure figure in the police records during this litany of confessions, time would soon change all that.

The authorities were stunned by what Fred was admitting to and claiming he had done alone, and before he had a chance to retract his statement, they put him into a pair of overalls similar to the ones the police themselves were wearing and ferried him back to Cromwell Street.

Fred walked in the front door like he had so many times before, except on this cold March day, everything was different. He led the authorities down into the 'bedroom' where Heather, Mae and Stephen had slept, cried, and been abused. It was the room that had once also been the cellar – a dark den in which so much violence had occurred.

With childish paintings on the half-plastered wall, an uneven floor dug up so many times, and the horrible smells seeping in through the pipes Fred had damaged from so much digging, the room could not have been a more extreme find for the police.

Fred pointed out various areas that they should explore and was then escorted back to jail shortly before midnight.

The next morning, the excavation resumed, this time in the cellar. The on-site team found themselves hacking away at hardened concrete, both hopeful and terrified that more bodies of the missing or forgotten would be found. And it did not take long before the first set of bones encased beneath the cellar was discovered.

It was the body of Therese Siegenthaler, the adventurous globe-trotting Swiss traveller who had saved up money from her part-time job in London while studying and was on her way to Ireland to meet a friend but had never arrived.

Instead, her body was found encased in concrete in front of a fake fireplace in the left-hand corner of the cellar. Next to her skull sat a knotted cloth, folded and rolled to form a loop.

Like so many other victims, the 21-year-old had been gagged and silenced in the moment she most desperately needed help to arrive.

***

Three hours later, Fred West was bundled into a police vehicle. Cuffed and with a blank face, he sat quietly while the van made its way across a stretch of seventeen miles before pulling in at a place that Fred knew like the back of his hand.

It was the village of Much Marcle, the scene of Fred's earliest gruesome deeds, and it was here where he now directed the police to Fingerpost Field and then told them to stop. They walked a short way towards the clump of trees known as Yewtree Coppice. Fred indicated what the police media statement would later call 'an area of interest', and the crew got to work.

It was here where the remains of Rena Costello, Fred's first wife with whom he had been in a tempestuous relationship, were discovered. All those years of breaking up and getting back together, Charmaine and Anne Marie being shuffled in and out of state care every other month, and the daring escape by Rena and Isa all those years ago, had come to this: Rena's remains lying undisturbed in a pastoral green meadow for twenty years, with nobody ever having searched for her.

When they uncovered Rena's body, they discovered a short length of metal tubing nearby, which seemed to indicate that

Fred had sexually assaulted her, either before or after he killed her, and had then extensively dismembered her body, putting the pieces into plastic bags and burying them.

This was a woman he had once 'loved' and who would have still been alive, after her daring escape, had she not come back in search of her children.

***

Fred was out in Fingerpost Field marking the spot where his wife's dismembered body was buried when the team back at Cromwell Street discovered the body of Shirley Hubbard, the youngest of their victims. The last time anyone had seen the fifteen-year-old girl, she had been waiting for a bus in the winter of 1974. This was after a day spent working at Debenhams, followed by a visit to the fun fair with her boyfriend. Now this same girl, it had come to light, had probably been offered a lift by the Wests and had been happy to skip the cold bus ride home.

Instead, she had ended up in the so-called house of horrors, brutally raped and tortured before being killed. And the most heartbreaking part of all: when Shirley was discovered in a part of the cellar that the West family called 'the Marilyn Monroe section' for some bizarre reason that nobody knows, it was found that her head had been encased in thick brown tape, the type used to securely wrap parcels. This had been wound round her head up to twelve times, after which thin plastic tubing was inserted through two holes and bent up towards her nasal cavity so that she could still breathe. Bluntly put, they had kept her alive for no other reason than to torture her further.

Like many others, nobody had ever gone looking for her, and her dreadful demise at the hands of the Wests would never have been discovered were it not for the police activity that was now unfolding twenty years too late.

ONE HORRIFIC FIND AFTER ANOTHER

With every new discovery, the media frenzy grew with each passing day. Such was the incredible nature of the evidence that soon, even news stations from outside the United Kingdom were flying reporters to the scene unfolding in Gloucester. Crowds of ordinary people gathered outside the house to gaze in wonder and horror at the facade and wait breathlessly for the police to appear with another box of remains to be taken to the lab for identification.

For the families who had endured years of missing loved ones, these days were torture. Some wanted closure, while others crumpled under the weight of having a daughter or sister be the victim in a gruesome drama that was playing out on an international stage.

***

Marian Partington, Lucy's sister, was 26 at the time of Lucy's disappearance at age 21 in 1973. After two decades of not knowing what happened to her sister, she was sitting at work in early March 1994 when she lifted up a newspaper and her blood ran cold.

There on the pages in front of her was a developing story about a couple called the Wests, whose house in Gloucester had become the focus of an ongoing excavation after the bodies of several young women had been found buried beneath mud and concrete. The rest of her family had also seen the papers, and the whole family had a sense that their beloved Lucy might have fallen victim to this same couple.

She called her mother and asked her to phone the police to remind them of the case from just over two decades before. Unlike many of the other victims, Lucy was from a well-to-do and close-knit family that had not given up looking for her after she disappeared from a bus stop after visiting a friend on Boxing Day.

Marian had already figured out that the Wests lived on the bus route that would have taken Lucy from her friend's place back to the family home on the night she never arrived back.

The very next day after phoning the incident room, Lucy's mother got the phone call no mother wanted to get: they had news for her. And from there, Marian would later say, everything felt like it 'went into slow motion'.

Lucy's body had not yet been found, but the police told Marian and her mother that Fred West had been talking to them and admitted more bodies were buried in the basement. He had mentioned that one of the young women there was named Lucy.

It was shortly after that, on Sunday 6 March, that the mystery that had haunted Lucy's family was finally solved for good, albeit with the worst possible outcome. At 9 a.m. on that cold morning in March, the team at 25 Cromwell Street came across her remains and from there were able to work out the excruciating end she had experienced. With two pieces of cord knotted together below her jaw, she too had not been able to yell for help.

And then, as if he and Rosemary had not brought enough misery upon the Partington family, they now had to endure Fred's outlandish fantasies claiming that he had actually known Lucy and that they were in a relationship.

Nothing could have been further from the truth: Lucy had inhabited an entirely different world from Fred West, and were it not for a chance moment of being at a certain bus stop on a certain day at a certain time, her life would not have been cut short as it was. She would, instead, have gone on to finish her English degree at university, with her whole adult life ahead of her.

***

Marian was not the only sister whose shattered world would fall apart even further with the excavations at 25 Cromwell Street. Juanita Mott's sister was watching the news on television when she had the same out-of-body experience as Marian. She immediately knew that her sister was likely a victim in this same chain of crimes and that Juanita's remains might be found at this address.

In the intervening years since 1975, Juanita's sister Belinda had followed every possible lead to try to find her. The last time anyone had seen her was when she was supposed to babysit a friend's child on the day of the friend's wedding. When she hadn't turned up, those close to her sighed in frustration: Juanita, eighteen years old, was always a bit rebellious, and perhaps this was just another expression of her independence.

But as the days rolled on, her sister Belinda had grown increasingly worried about her.

A deathly silence and the pain of her sister's mysterious absence had haunted Belinda for nineteen years. After months of trying to find her, she had finally given up and had attempted to live as normal a life as possible, but she was forever haunted by her sister's disappearance.

And now she would finally get the truth, if not a comforting closure.

Juanita's body was found just three hours after Lucy's. She had been buried beneath the staircase that led from this cold torture chamber up to the main section of the house. She was identified by her dental records and after the forensic dentist was able to reconstruct her cheekbones. Like so many of the others, there were bones missing from Juanita's body, including fingers and toes. She had also been decapitated and her head had been struck by a heavy object – probably when Fred was trying to get it into a hole. It was clear from the evidence that before she died, a band of fabric had been pulled around her lower jaw and around the back of her head. Around the other remaining parts of her body, a rope covered in plastic was tangled up.

Her sister, horrified by these facts, found a tiny modicum of consolation in the fact that Juanita was tough and would have fought back with everything she had. 'If there were any scratches on Fred West, just know they were put there by Juanita,' she would say about her sister.

On Monday 7 March, the day after Lucy's and Juanita's remains had been found, the four bodies excavated from the cellar thus far were removed from Cromwell Street by Professor Knight. What these victims had craved more than anything in their last brutal hours of life, they were now granted in death: to leave the house of horrors behind them.

That same day, Fred was back in the Gloucester Magistrates' Court, where he was remanded in custody for another four days while investigations continued, and that very afternoon, Lynda Gough's remains were finally found.

This meant that yet another family had had their worst nightmare confirmed, but only after 21 years of the hell of not knowing.

Lynda had been the first victim that Fred and Rose assaulted together after being caught for assaulting Caroline Owens and getting away with a small fine. Lynda had been abducted only three months after Caroline and after the Wests had realised that it was too risky to let anyone live after they had seen and felt what Fred and Rose were capable of.

The details around Lynda's death were horrific. She had been suspended from wooden beams in the cellar, and her head had been wrapped in adhesive and surgical tape to silence her screams. Like Shirley Hubbard after her, small tubes had been inserted into her nose so she could breathe and stay alive while they tortured her. She had then died either through suffocation or strangulation once they tired of her. The body that was retrieved from under the concrete floor that Monday afternoon was missing five cervical vertebrae, the patellae and numerous finger bones.

Along with other family members, Lynda Gough's mother, who had never understood why her child had cut contact with the family, would now live with the nightmare of knowing the truth.

***

As if Monday 7 March 1994 had not been eventful enough, with four bodies having been removed from the scene, Fred West being remanded in custody for a further four days, and another body found in the afternoon, more was still to come.

At around 7 p.m. that evening, with the sun long set and the air growing increasingly cold, Fred was ushered into a police van once more.

There he sat in the vehicle as the police carted him back to Fingerpost Field in a bid to find the remains of Anne McFall. In true bizarre Fred fashion, he was happy to admit that he knew her and where her body might be, but denied killing her. His claims of innocence regarding her death made no sense, and all the police could do was continue their search for her body in a large open field more than two decades after it had been buried. This was no easy task in such a big area and the initial search yielded no results.

Twenty-four hours passed before another body was uncovered back at Cromwell Street. This time it was the remains of Carole Ann Cooper. She was the young girl of fifteen who ended up in a children's home after her mother passed away and her father divorced her stepmother a few years later.

She had last been seen in November 1973 after watching a movie with her boyfriend and friends and going out for a drink in Brickfields Road. She had waved goodbye at the bus stop as her companions walked off, but then never arrived at her grandmother's house where she was meant to stay that night.

It is highly likely that the Wests found her waiting at the bus stop and offered her a lift. By the time her grandmother began to panic when she failed to arrive, Carole Ann was likely already in the cellar at Cromwell Street, being raped and tortured.

The evidence showed that, like Lynda Gough before her, Carole Ann had been suspended from the beams of the cellar with her face covered in surgical tape. She was tortured until she died of asphyxiation. Fred had pointed out where her remains could be found and referred to Carole Ann as the 'Worcester girl'. Still wrapped around her skull was an elasticated cloth band that had been wound around her jaw to keep her silent.

***

Over the next few days, lots of equipment, including ground-penetrating radar, was delivered to Fingerpost Field in the hope that it would be useful for the Home Office pathologist and other professionals who had become involved in the search for Anne McFall.

Meanwhile, on Thursday 10 March 1994, eight of the nine sets of remains that had been discovered were transferred to the College of Medicine at the University of Wales in Cardiff, where Professor Bernard Knight, a government forensic pathologist, had the gruesome task of figuring out what the remains would prove.

In essence, eight young women and girls who had been brutally murdered were now a collection of bones that needed to be analysed as if they were scientific specimens. Only through this intricate process could the forensic evidence be properly scrutinised – and the outcomes were devastating. They showed not only a modus operandi that was repeated over and over again, but they also showed the extent to which the Wests had treated their victims as disposable toys for their own sadistic pleasure.

All the victims, apart from Heather and Shirley Robinson, had been silenced with man-made masks or gags around their heads or mouths. The bereft family members of these victims, apart from everything else, had to now imagine their loved ones not being able to call for help and experiencing extreme pain in silence.

The burials had been as brutal as the murders themselves. Most of the victims, Knight would later tell the court, had been decapitated and dismembered, and many had bones missing. Legs had been parted from hip joints, and the Wests' victims were buried in graves too cramped for a full body to be laid flat and in one piece. Knight found that in the case of most victims, either one or both knee caps had been removed, as had wrists, toes, fingers and ankle bones. Many of the bones had also been cut with a sharp knife, and in the case of Lucy Partington, who had 72 bones missing, a knife was found inside the grave.

Despite the growing catalogue of gruesome discoveries and the ongoing burden on Knight to uncover the full extent of what had happened, Fred West was not put in prison at this point. Instead, he was remanded in custody and kept available to assist the police locate the remains of other victims.

By the middle of March, investigations at Cromwell Street were beginning to slow down. With all the digging and excavation, the police began to worry that the entire structure had become unstable. In an echo of Fred's own past, the authorities poured six square metres of concrete into the basement to try and stabilise the foundations while they continued their work.

People still gathered at the scene, however, to gaze at a place now synonymous with murder and destruction but which, in reality, was just an empty shell of a house.

Rose, meanwhile, was moved to a new detention facility in Dursley, while a new search warrant was soon signed and sealed, this time to trawl through the address of 25 Midland Road, where the Wests had lived with Charmaine and Anne Marie before moving to Cromwell Street.

***

In April of 1994, the investigation team turned their attention to Rose West's role in all of the killings. Fred had tried his best to shield her from questioning but the sheer scale of the inquiry and the number of bodies retrieved made it very hard to imagine she was not involved. On 24 April, Rose was formally charged with the murder of Lynda Gough, and she replied with only two words: 'I'm innocent.'

Over and over again, that was her reply as the charges piled up over the coming days. Carole Ann Cooper, Lucy Partington, Therese Siegenthaler; she listened stony-faced and then replied by saying, 'I'm innocent.'

The morning after concrete was poured into 25 Cromwell Street and the police turned their gaze to Midland Road, Fred handed a strange note to the interviewers with whom he had spent so much time over the last few months. It read: 'I have not and still cannot tell you the whole truth … from the very first day of this enquiry my main concern has been to protect another person or persons.' There was little to no doubt he was referring to Rose, but it would not take long before her name too was yoked to some of the gruesome crimes Britain had seen in its modern history.

On Tuesday 3 May, those already traumatised from working on the case returned to the scene of Midland Road after the sweet relief of the bank holiday the day before. Now the council engineers arrived, ready to dig up the kitchen of the house, wondering if it, too, was a solid graveyard filled with human remains and concrete.

When the excavations first began, nothing was found.

The next day, however, would prove to be an eventful one. In the late afternoon, Rose was formally charged with the murder of Shirley Hubbard, and this time she made no reply. This woman, who had once blown her top with anger on an almost daily basis, now stood quietly as her charge sheet grew longer and longer.

It was at seven that evening when a new discovery would thrust her even further into the spotlight from which Fred had tried to shield her.

Officers excavating the kitchen at 25 Midland Road happened upon human remains, just as they had expected they might.

Once again, Professor Bernard Knight was tasked with excavating the site to safely remove the remains so they could be tested for forensic purposes. They were transported to the College of Medicine at the University of Wales in Cardiff, just like the remains of the nine victims found in Cromwell Street.

This time, it was not the skeletons of those on the brink of womanhood or who had already grown up. Instead, they were the remains of a petite little girl, and soon, the forensic evidence would prove that this is what had become of Charmaine West, the spirited child who had only ever been searched for by her own mother after she disappeared into thin air and who had always been missed by her little sister, Anne Marie.

For the public, already aghast at what had been found in Cromwell Street, the knowledge that another one of the children in the Wests' care had been murdered at a different site sent shockwaves across the media. Little Charmaine was neither Fred nor Rose's biological daughter. She had, instead, been caught in the tempestuous storm of Fred and Rena's acrimonious parting all those years ago outside a caravan in a trailer park.

Over all those years, Anne Marie had been gaslit by her father Fred and stepmother Rose into believing that her mother Rena had abandoned her and that her sister Charmaine had just left one day with no warning.

Years later, in her autobiography, Anne Marie would recall the devastation of being told after school one day that her big sister had been collected by their mother but that she was going to stay behind.

She described how she had asked why only her sister was collected by Rena and not her, and Fred had responded, 'She wouldn't want you. You're the wrong colour.'

Now, when the truth had finally come to light, all the abuse and sexual violence she had endured made more sense in light of what had been revealed: her father and stepmother were not just cruel rapists, they were monstrous murderers who, between them, had killed her mother and two of her sisters, Charmaine and Heather, along with so many other young women and girls.

Not only that, Charmaine, far from being elsewhere with her mother, was actually deceased and buried right below the kitchen in the very flat in which they had lived. Police believed Rose had murdered little Charmaine while Fred was still in prison and had then placed her body in the coal cellar. When Fred walked through the gates of the prison and was back home in Midland Road, he took care of 'the problem' for his wife.

The horror was compounded by the news that Charmaine's body, like so many of the other victims, had been severed at the hip. Fred, however, was adamant that he had not dismembered her. Instead, he claimed that his stepdaughter's body had been 'damaged' when he had undertaken renovations on the property years after the family had moved out and that she had definitely been buried intact. However, like with almost all the other victims, bones were missing from the fingers, toes, ankles and kneecaps. This gave rise to speculation that they had been retained as some kind of macabre souvenirs.

***

Investigations and excavations continued for the remainder of May that year, and by month end, police were satisfied that no other human remains were to be found in the Cromwell Street or Midland Road house.

Early in June, the notorious House of Horrors case was on the lips of every Briton and many others all over the world. And when Fred appeared at the local magistrates' court once more, nine of the murder charges had been amended to include the name of Rosemary West as an accused.

Later that same day, the unsuspecting owners of 25 Midland Road, whose lives had been turned upside down by an excavation in the kitchen, could now take possession of their house once again. But with that return came the dreadful knowledge that a girl of eight had been murdered, dismembered and buried in concrete in that very kitchen some two decades earlier.

A few days later, after another gruelling session of searching the vast green expanse of Fingerpost Field in the mild heat of June, police diggers were about to pack away their equipment and head home to their families. But then, at around 6.22 p.m., they made the discovery they had been hoping for.

There lay the remains of a young teenager who had died more than two decades earlier. Next to her lay the remains of her unborn child.

The remains, as expected, proved to be those of Anne McFall and the baby she had conceived with Fred West.

This was a young teenager who had once loved Fred and stayed with him when Isa and Rena had fled. She had almost carried his baby to term but was murdered weeks before she was due to give birth.

Fred would later claim that he stabbed her to death during a heated argument, but around her wrists were the remains of a dressing gown belt, and, like so many of the others, finger bones were missing and her body had been dismembered.

The entire dark saga of Fred West and his serial killing, which began on his own and ended with his partner in crime, Rose West, had now come full circle.

The two murderers had not laid eyes on each other since February of 1994, but they were scheduled to appear in court together on June 30. For so long, their relationship had existed in the shadows, but on that date, the eyes of the world would be watching.

And as for the bereft, those whose lives had been shattered by the disappearance of loved ones decades before and then shattered all over again by the horrific discoveries, there was no reprieve.

It was only the heartbreaking image of Marian Partington, Lucy's sister, that could perhaps act as a symbolic placeholder for all those on whose lives Fred and Rose had left an indelible mark by killing their loved ones.

Marian wanted to see Lucy's remains for herself and bring back some humanity to the jumble of bones that had once been her sister.

She had been dreaming about putting her arms around a skeleton for many years, and in the dream, the bones became flesh. After Lucy was found, Marian knew she wanted to see the remains. So she gathered up two of Lucy's teddy bears from when she was a baby, plus her soft brown blanket (her 'snuggler'), and made her way to her sister's remains. She asked for the coffin to be opened.

Cradling Lucy's skull, the shape of which she easily and lovingly recognised, she placed her lips on the brow and gave her sister one last kiss. She then wrapped it in the soft brown snuggler, placed her teddy bears beside her, and said goodbye.

'It's the most profound thing I have ever done in my life,' she would later say.

Lucy was finally laid to rest on 16 February 1995.

16

The End Of Fred

In the summer of 1994, there had been a brief lull in the progression of the case through the legal system. The murder of Anne McFall had been added to the list of charges that Fred was facing, 27 years after her mysterious disappearance when she was only eighteen years old and pregnant with Fred's child.

There were still three weeks to go before Fred and Rose were scheduled to appear in court together. Partners in crime for so many years with so much torture inflicted on others, they had not seen each other for four months. Fred was lost without Rose and was likely anticipating the frisson of them seeing one another again, albeit in the halls of justice. Rose, on the other hand, was cooking up new ways to try to dismantle the scales of justice.

A young barrister, Sasha Wass, had taken on her case. With a sharp mind, and fox-like features to match, Wass had the cool hand that was needed in a case like this, a case that had rocked the country with its sordid details and harrowing tales of torture.

She was a busy Londoner at the time and was only at the start of what would become a sterling career both defending and prosecuting in some rather high-profile cases, including that of actor Johnny Depp and Australian TV personality Rolf Harris. But back in 1994, she was very much a junior in the profession.

She had seen headlines about bodies being discovered in a builder's garden, but she had hardly taken up a front row seat in the media circus surrounding the case. One day, her senior clerk asked her to pay a visit to the Pucklechurch Remand Centre. She would later describe that moment to Howard Sounes for the *Fred and Rose West Tapes* podcast: 'My senior clerk asked me if I would go visit somebody who was in custody at Pucklechurch Remand Centre. I said yes. He knew about the case and was having a bit of a joke with me. He said "a case called West". I knew that there were bodies found in the garden but that was about it.'

Over the next days, Wass immersed herself in the case, brushing up on every aspect of a criminal case that was harrowing and unfinished in equal measure. She was, as expected, horrified by the details after reading up on one victim after the other and what the excavations at both Cromwell Street and Midland Road had shown. She remained, however, committed to the principle that everyone deserves a fair trial and a robust defence. And so she began figuring out her approach.

Her client, Rose West, had spent several months behind the heavy-duty metal doors of the remand centre, likely thinking of little else than what prospects lay ahead for her. The public, over those months, had held its collective breath, waiting to pounce on the story when it came back onto the court roll.

And so it was that by the morning of 30 June, Rose and her counsel had settled on a strategy and were ready to begin presenting it in a courtroom tucked behind the dour facade of the magistrates' court in Gloucester.

Fred had been consistent in his attempts to shield Rose from blame, despite the absurdity of imagining she knew nothing about what was going on in and below her own home. He likely expected their dark bond to be reignited in the courtroom as they set eyes on each other after a long separation, and that this connection would overshadow the workings of the courtroom. Or at the very least, he likely expected some loyalty from Rose, especially in light of his attempts to spare her.

But the moment Rose West appeared in the courtroom at the magistrates' court, she made no eye contact with him. She didn't even acknowledge his presence and simply stared ahead as if he were a stranger.

Fred was being represented by a solicitor called Howard Ogden, who was up close in the courthouse when the two were brought together. He saw the moment Fred gazed lovingly at Rose, and caught his confusion when she wouldn't even look back at him. Then Ogden saw Fred lean over and whisper something to her and place his hand on her shoulder. Rose winced visibly and withdrew and Fred reacted as if he'd been stung.

'She was stony-faced and cold and that was a big shock to Fred,' Ogden would later say about that moment. 'He thought she would be desperate to embrace him and be so grateful for taking the rap but in fact she was hoping to save her own neck.'

The teenage girl who had once spurned the advances of an older man at a bus stop in early 1969 was now giving him the cold shoulder in court, with more than ten other young women and girls dead in the intervening years.

The author Geoffrey Wansell, who was also present that day in court, simply added, 'She was unmoved. She had written him off.'

It was at this same hearing that Fred, charged with eleven counts of murder since Anne McFall was added as a victim, was remanded in custody to police cells for three days until Monday 4 July 1994.

Rose, charged with nine counts of murder and other sexual offences, was remanded in custody until Thursday 28 July 1994.

Before he was led away from the hearing, Fred made one more attempt to connect with Rose, but as he moved towards her, she shrank away from his outstretched hand and turned her back on him.

This moment snapped something in him and seemed to loosen a pathological bond that had seen Rose and Fred commit the most dastardly of crimes together. The shock of the rejection had a physical effect on Fred's whole demeanour. After that, he stopped cooperating with the police. No longer spurred on by his fervour to protect Rose, all he could muster was the simple phrase 'no comment'.

For Rose, the fallout was practical rather than psychological. As the evidence stacked up against her, she no longer had an accomplice shielding her by single-handedly assuming responsibility for all that had happened.

Over the course of the next few months, Fred and Rose would see each other at hearings at the magistrates' court, but since that first time she had snubbed him, Rose did not change her cold demeanour towards him a single time.

As the days dragged into weeks and the trial drew closer, Fred's mental condition deteriorated. It was reported that he showed signs of paranoia. Even he could not figure out the tangled web of lies he had woven as he became increasingly unsure of what he had said when and to whom. His defence lawyer, Howard Ogden, was the person left trying to untangle it all, but he would soon be fired by Fred amid allegations that Ogden was planning to cash in on the information he had gleaned from Fred as his client.

The two men had travelled quite a journey together, with Ogden sometimes reeling from what he'd been told and at other times allegedly joking around with his client about the movie they would make together about the murders.

One poignant moment that Ogden would later share in a documentary was when he first heard Fred confess to the murder of his daughter, Heather. This was in the presence of the investigating officers too. Ogden recalled: 'We were dealing with an account the likes of which none of us had ever heard or dealt with before in our professions.'

It was such a chilling moment that a very unusual thing then happened: Ogden, the lead detective and the two investigating officers all got up and one by one walked into a small cupboard area that doubled as a tearoom. There, stunned by what they heard and how coldly it had been told, they spontaneously put their arms around each other in a silent group hug.

Now, a few months later, Fred and his lawyer were parting company and Fred was bringing on a new pair of attorneys called Bobbetts and Mackan. Rose's rejection had come at the same time as his children wanting nothing to do with him.

Rose, it seems, was still hanging her hopes on portraying herself as another of Fred's victims rather than being his equally sadistic accomplice, and a committal hearing was set for February 1995 where the court would decide whether the evidence was sufficient to put the accused on trial by jury.

For most of 1994 after his arrest, Fred had been placed on suicide watch. This meant that he was under constant surveillance, was kept away from any dangerous objects, and had no access to materials or objects that could be shaped into a noose, since hanging is the most common suicide method in incarceration.

THE END OF FRED

On 29 November, Rose's birthday, he wrote a suicide note that he addressed to Rose, Stephen and Mae, and all through December, he made no attempt to take his own life. But it became clear that when families across the country were huddled around the fireplace opening Christmas gifts, Fred was still plotting his escape – not from prison but from his own existence. It was around that time that officials surveilling the prisoners on suicide watch were thin on the ground, and Fred spotted an opportunity.

On New Year's Day 1995, with the prison guards distracted and recovering from their celebrations, he saw his opportunity. Despite their best attempts, the officials had not accounted for Fred fashioning a rope out of blankets and an assortment of tags he had stolen off the prison laundry bags, and come the first day of the year, he gathered up this rope he had been fashioning in his cell and quickly wrapped it around his own neck. He then tied it around a door handle and window catchment. The man who had tortured so many others was now robbing his own body of its lifeforce. He fell to his knees and waited until he could breathe no more.

***

When Fred West died on New Year's Day 1995, he did so without ever facing the consequences of what he had done. He also did so without facing the families whose lives he had ruined or shedding light on the many other victims he claimed he had killed.

Less than a year had passed between his arrest as a suspect in Heather's murder and him taking his own life. In the intervening months, while the story had cooled off a little in the absence of dramatic moments, the horrific details that came out at the time of the excavations were still fresh in the public mind. Fred was not the only West who had died by hanging that year. His brother John, while on trial for rape, had hung himself in the garage at his home, days before the jury was set to return with a verdict in his case. John's crimes were always overshadowed by his older brother's, but that doesn't make them any less horrific or harmful to his many victims, including Anne Marie, whom he had raped over three hundred times during the course of her childhood.

News of Fred's death spread rapidly around the world, bringing with it outrage that the authorities had failed in their duties to prevent this. It meant that one of Britain's cruellest citizens in modern history had evaded justice once again.

There was, however, one person who seemed to take much delight in his death, and that was Rose, his wife, accomplice and mother of some of his children.

Rose's solicitor, Leo Goatley, would later describe the moment when Rose received the news of Fred's death. 'There was a certain glow and relief in her expression,' he recalled. Also present when Rose got the news was the prison supervisor at HM Prison Birmingham, where she was being held. Her name was Vanessa Frake, and she recalled the moment simply by saying, 'There was no emotion there at all.'

The last time the murderers had clapped eyes on each other was 13 December, two weeks prior, when they had appeared once more at Gloucester Magistrates' Court. Again, Rose had acted like Fred was a complete stranger, and when they were both remanded in custody and a committal hearing fixed for 6 February the next year at Dursley Magistrates' Court, Rose had remained poker-faced.

Now, as the year was just beginning and with the committal hearing just over a month away, Rose's fate hung in the balance. With Fred gone and little forensic evidence to pin the murders on her, Rose might have imagined she'd be getting away with it thanks to his passing.

While Rose might have registered 'relief', as per her solicitor's description, about Fred taking his own life, he had gone into death still clinging to the macabre connection the two of them shared.

His suicide note read:

To Rose West, Steve and Mae,

Well Rose it's your birthday on 29 November 1994 and you will be 41 and still beautiful and still lovely and I love you. We will always be in love.

The most wonderful thing in my life was when I met you. Our love is special to us. So, love, keep your promises to me. You know what they are. Where we are put together for ever and ever is up to you. We loved Heather, both of us. I would love Charmaine to be with Heather and Rena.

You will always be Mrs. West, all over the world. That is important to me and to you.

I haven't got you a present, but all I have is my life. I will give it to you, my darling. When you are ready, come to me. I will be waiting for you.

He had drawn a gravestone at the bottom of the letter and on the stone, it said: 'In loving memory. Fred West. Rose West. Rest in peace where no shadow falls. In perfect peace he waits for Rose, his wife.'

Four months to the day after he penned the suicide note, Fred West was cremated in secret at Canley Crematorium in Coventry. Residents of the city commuting home that day sat clutching copies of the *Coventry Evening Telegraph*, on the front of which was splashed a photograph of Fred West grinning like he owned the world.

His body had been taken from his cell in Winson Green prison to a mortuary in Birmingham, where it was kept on ice for three months and then transported to Coventry.

The funeral lasted only a few minutes. There were no flowers, no hymns, and certainly no eulogies about the life of the deceased man. Only one son and one daughter attended, though their names were not shared with the public. And though it isn't written in any public record, it is believed his ashes were scattered in the Welsh seaside resort of Barry Island.

17

The Trial

Detective Superintendent John Bennett had the career-defining task of being in charge of the West serial murder case. Exasperated by the public hunger for more stories, and the media machine feeding that hunger, he sat down to pen a statement that he hoped would put a stop to it ahead of the upcoming hearing on whether there was enough evidence to warrant a trial. It read: 'The case against Mrs West must not be prejudiced by irresponsible reporting from the media. That's the end of that.'

His greatest concern was an unethical ecosystem in which newspapers bought stories from witnesses and splashed them across the front pages, thus prejudicing the prosecution's case.

Sasha Wass, Rose's lawyer, felt the same way. Years later, she would tell journalist Howard Sounes how Rose had been 'vilified in the press after the death of her husband'.

She added, 'The spotlight turned from him to her. So many reports had been circulated that it would prejudice a jury and she would no longer be able to get a fair trial.'

The first hearing after Fred's death was scheduled for early February in the village of Dursley. The press descended on the sleepy village, transforming it overnight into a hive of activity round the clock. As the trial drew nearer, press vans carrying journalists were trundling down the narrow roads, and curious onlookers, desperate to be part of the action, descended on the courthouse. In a macabre twist of fate, the unremarkable dowdy woman who had lived in obscurity in a semi was now the centre of attention for all the wrong reasons, and everyone would try to catch a glimpse of the woman they believed to be one of the most evil killers in history.

The frenzy was so intense that, as Rose made her way into town, children lined up along the side of the road and pelted the van carrying her to the court with eggs, while others chanted, 'Burn her! Burn her!'

Detective Bennett already seemed depleted and like he owed the public an explanation for what was about to happen. Going into the hearing on the first day, he said, 'If the worst case plays out and she gets off, we've done our best. Wasn't our fault.'

Wass, for her part, knew that the chances of the charges being dropped in the face of insufficient evidence to warrant a trial were slim.

'I knew when I was at court I was pushing an elephant up the hill, but that doesn't stop you from putting forward the argument. But from a non-lawyer point of view, there's no doubt that the public wanted closure,' she would later recall.

The court laid down the condition that the reporters would only be allowed to report on the names of the lawyers, the accused and the magistrate. They could also list the victims and state whether legal aid was granted or not. But beyond that, nothing was permitted by way of reporting. The temptation would be high for any journalist worth their salt to jot down every detail, and certainly, the millions following the case would have welcomed such information. But the conditions were set and nothing could be done. And so, the many journalists and photographers moving about the town grabbed onto anything they could to build a story, but there wasn't much there.

A countrywide frisson was building as the chief magistrate, Peter Badge, deliberated over his decision on whether a trial would go ahead. With the population of the market town of Dursley swelling up with journalists, Badge carefully considered both sides, and then, on Valentine's Day, he announced his decision: Rosemary West was committed for trial on ten counts of murder and other charges that she had not previously faced.

The trial was set to begin nine months later, on 3 October 1995, at Winchester Crown Court.

***

When that day arrived, the frenzy that had abated over the quieter months suddenly roared back to life, making Dursley seem like a country picnic. Over two hundred journalists jostled for space outside the courtroom. Photographers had their lenses trained on the street where Rose would be arriving, and reporters had their pens poised above their notepads, waiting to scribble down whatever they saw when the moment arrived.

Rose was being held at the Winchester prison and would make the short drive to the court in a police van with tinted windows, a drive that no doubt took her from the isolation of her cell to the intense gaze of the world.

The police knew what to expect and had held meetings to plan accordingly. Now the day was upon them, and exactly as they anticipated, Rose's arrival at the court thickened the rind of reporters and onlookers who'd been gathered for several hours.

It was barely five minutes later, after exiting the police vehicle, that Rose had settled into her seat in court number three, wearing a dark skirt and jacket with a white blouse underneath.

Her fringe hung over her large round glasses and she wore a small cross around her neck.

The judge assigned to the case was Charles Mantell, a highly regarded man in the criminal justice system who had been appointed as a high court judge five years prior and whose appointment was sealed with a knighthood. Known for his calm demeanour and kindness, he was just the right person to preside over a trial that would bring the most harrowing details into the public domain.

The man leading the prosecution would be the formidable Brian Leveson. Like Mantell, he was tailor-made for his role in this particular serial murder case, one that was not going to be easy either in terms of the gruesome picture that would be painted of 25 Cromwell Street or the forensic evidence to prove Rose's part in all of it.

Leading Rose's defence team would be the well-known barrister Richard Ferguson and his junior, Sasha Wass. Ferguson was a barrister from Northern Ireland who had been elected to the parliament of Northern Ireland in 1968 during the height of the country's turmoil and was frequently subjected to intimidation. He stood down in 1971 citing 'ill health' and turned his attention to the law, then moved to London in 1986 and became a QC.

It was up to Wass to kick off the proceedings, and she stated, 'There is no direct evidence against Mrs West at all. Nobody saw her ever involved with abusing any of the people whose remains were later found in Cromwell Street, nobody saw her dismembering bodies, nobody saw her even having anything to do with most of them, and of course she constantly denied any involvement and there was no forensic evidence either.'

Her stance was that the prosecution had a steep hill to climb.

Brian Leveson, not surprisingly, held a sharply contrasting view and pulled no punches in saying so. In his opening statement, he said that the human remains found at Cromwell Street and Midland Road portrayed something 'more terrible than words can express'. He began building his picture of the West couple as sadistic maniacs and said the victims' 'last moments on earth were as objects of the sexual depravity of this woman and her husband'.

He said, 'Each (victim) was dumped without decency or respect in a different hole some three feet below the ground in the garden, in the cellar, or underneath a bathroom. One of the victims carried a foetus in its ninth month of gestation.'

That set the tone for what would unfold in the courtroom, day after day, and as he foreshadowed right at the outset, what those in the courtroom would be hearing over the following days and weeks circumstantial evidence that was more than sufficient to illustrate Rose's guilt.

So much of what was found in the Cromwell Street house and further afield was already information in the public domain, and still, as the trial unfolded, few were prepared for the stories of cruelty and horror that would be painted in fine detail.

Paul Stokes, a journalist from London, would later say that those present 'were not spared of any of the graphic details of what had become of those poor girls'. He said the 'pathological evidence' presented in court 'pointed to some form of sadistic behaviour against them while they were still alive, culminating in their deaths'.

Journalist Jackie Storer would later recall the experience in a column she wrote for the BBC's online news publication ten years after covering the trial.

'For seven harrowing weeks my colleagues on the press benches and I sat and listened to the most incredible story of depravity, sexual obsession and sheer evil. None of us had an inkling about how bad it was going to be.'

What she described as one of the 'many moments of high drama' was when a tape recording of Fred's interview with the police was played to the jury.

This, which only came at a late stage in the trial, would be the first time the voice of Rose's dead accomplice was heard in the courtroom.

'His thick West Country accent evident, and speaking in the most matter-of-fact way, this cheerful-sounding little man described how he murdered and cut up their own daughter Heather. He said she had wanted to leave home, he lunged at her, strangled her and chopped her up with an ice saw. He finally buried her body under the patio. According to him, Rose was out shopping at the time.'

Storer recalled how she rushed out to file his exact words for the afternoon edition of her paper.

'Reading them back from my notebook to my colleague, who was copy-taking, it was impossible to believe this was a father talking about his daughter.'

***

The strongest weapon in the prosecution's artillery would prove to be their reliance on something called 'similar fact evidence'. This concept, used in criminal and civil trials, is when evidence shows that an accused has behaved in a similar way in the past under circumstances that are similar to those in the current case. The idea is that such evidence may demonstrate a pattern of behaviour, which could be relevant to proving the facts at issue in the current case.

Enter Caroline Owens, the only victim who had unwittingly walked through the doors of the House of Horrors and had also left the house still alive.

THE TRIAL

That was back in 1972, after which the Wests had pleaded guilty to indecent assault and causing actual bodily harm. At the time, as described earlier in this book, Caroline had settled for the lesser charge of assault because of her reluctance to endure public scrutiny about her life.

Now, 23 years later, she would prove to be the star witness for the prosecution and had an opportunity to erase at least some of the deep regret she had harboured all those years prior for not telling the full story of what the Wests had done to her.

Now, as a woman of 39, she walked towards the witness stand with none of the fear that had stymied her testimony in the early 1970s. She still had her cropped fringe across her forehead, but in the place of the dimple-cheeked seventeen-year-old in the high fashion clothes of two decades earlier, she now cut a more confident figure.

With hair back in a neat bun and two pearl earrings on the sides of her womanly face, a tailored jacket and a white shirt, she took those present back to the worst night of her life as she described the full extent of the horrors visited upon her at the hands of Rose and Fred. The details she relayed tallied up with some of what the other victims, who never came out alive, had clearly experienced.

She described how the Wests had abducted her on the side of the road, then took her back to their house, where they held her prisoner all night. In graphic detail, she told the court how Fred had raped her and how Rosemary had viciously sexually assaulted her using the exact kinds of equipment that had been found with so many of the other victims.

She had also recalled her fear when the Wests got angry when she tried to make a noise to attract help, and said of Fred, 'He told me that he would keep me in the cellar and ... bury me under the paving stones of Gloucester.'

Wass would later explain to Howard Sounes about the prosecution's case: 'Given the fact that there was tape, bindings and rope found in the graves, they must have also been held hostage in the way that Caroline Owens was held hostage.'

Under cross-examination, Owens was composed right up until the end when she was asked if she had made a deal with the media.

She was forced to admit that a tabloid had paid her for her story. She broke down and admitted there was a deal but explained that all she wanted was to help the other girls who had gone through the same hell as her but had ended up losing their lives.

By the time she left the witness box at Winchester Crown Court, Owens was in tears but had done a great service for the prosecution.

She was one of sixty witnesses the prosecution had lined up. Among them was Daisy Letts, Rose's own mother. She appeared frail and overwhelmed by the courtroom atmosphere but managed to recount her story of Rose having appeared at the house all those years ago with a much older boyfriend about whom she had said to her parents, 'He is capable of anything, even murder.'

The implication for the jury was that Rose knew exactly what kind of a man she had married. Throughout her testimony, Daisy Letts never once looked at her daughter.

Another witness who provided damning testimony was a former neighbour from Midland Road called Elizabeth Agius, who testified that Fred had told her about the trips he and Rose would take, cruising the streets as far away as Bristol and London, looking for young girls they could recruit to be sex workers. Fred told her it was easier to do when Rose was with him. One day, when Elizabeth asked him where he was going, he simply said, 'I'm going to see what I can find and bring home.'

When June Gough stepped into the witness stand at the trial, her face had the same haunted look as many of the other parents and siblings who had endured years of pain before the human remains found in Cromwell Street made their worst nightmares real. With the eyes of each jury member fixed on her, she described how she had found Rose wearing her daughter's slippers, and the way that Rose had changed her story to explain why that was the case.

Also among the witnesses for the prosecution was Anne Marie, by then 31 years old and clearly still caught in the trap of feeling bad about hating her father and stepmother. Her emotional testimony was so harrowing, not only because of the details she shared but because of the flashes of tenderness she still exhibited for the stepmother who had wrecked her life and taken that of so many others.

From the witness stand, her voice was soft, almost trance-like, as she spoke about her life at 25 Cromwell Street. The years of sexual violence, emotional abuse, trauma and fear were etched on her face, no doubt made worse by the recent revelation that her mother and her two sisters, Charmaine and Heather, had been murdered.

Anne Marie, for the first time in her life, publicly stated the extreme violence of her childhood, about how the first time she was raped she was only eight years old and about how she was often strapped to a metal frame that Fred had welded while her parents raped her.

She shared how she'd been made to feel 'grateful' that they were teaching her about sex, even as her stepmother smirked and taunted her, and her descriptions of being gagged and bound fitted the exact picture painted by the forensic evidence found with the sets of human remains in the garden and cellar.

One of the saddest moments of all was Anne Marie's testimony of how her older sister Charmaine had chosen stoicism, 'refusing to cry' when Rose violently beat her, as she saw this as a sign of weakness.

All those in court sat spellbound – if heartbroken – by the authenticity of her testimony. Many would later describe how she looked at her stepmother with undisguised love and a persistent search for acceptance, a dynamic that made her testimony even more riveting.

Like the other children, Anne Marie had not witnessed her stepmother murdering anyone, but the testimony made it all the more believable that Rose was capable of extreme violence.

Sitting quietly in the gallery listening to this gut-wrenching testimony was Belinda Mott, sister of victim Juanita. Belinda grasped that a chance – and fatal – encounter with the murderous couple was matched by years of living under the same roof. On another day, Belinda saw Anne Marie and Stephen sitting to one side at the trial. She went over to speak to them. They were overwhelmed by this gesture and thanked her. They put their arms around her and held her in an embrace.

'You're as much a victim as we are,' Belinda told the siblings.

Anne Marie's testimony also shed light on the murder of Shirley Robinson.

The prosecution and defence had had very different theories about what had happened. The prosecution told the jury they believed Rose had killed her in a fit of jealous rage after discovering she was pregnant with Fred's child. The defence claimed Rose never believed Fred was the father and that he had told Rose he was pretending to have sired the baby to cover up for a respectable businessman who didn't want it revealed he had impregnated Shirley. In this version of events, things took a tragic turn when Shirley told Fred that she was going to tell

Rose it was his, and so he murdered her and buried her and the unborn baby on the family property.

Anne Marie took those in court behind the scenes of how Shirley's pregnancy had affected the dynamics in the house.

She said her father had taunted Rose about the baby and that Rose was angered. She said that life became very tense in the house because of this, and many a fight ensued.

'I came home from school one day very close to when Shirley's baby was due and I was told that Shirley had gone to Germany.'

Anne Marie never saw or heard about Shirley again, until her and her baby's remains were found on the property at 25 Cromwell Street.

What the prosecution had presented in the West case was essentially two groups of victims: those whose murders were sexually motivated, as evidenced by the presence of gags, tape and ligatures in their graves, and those victims who were problems that needed to be solved. The dead daughters, Charmaine and Heather, fell into the latter category.

In the case of Charmaine's murder, the prosecution wished to show the jury that Fred had nothing to do with it and that the dental evidence could prove Fred was in jail when Charmaine was murdered.

Journalist Jackie Storer would later describe this heartbreaking moment, which brought home the humanity that sat behind dental evidence. This evidence, revealing as it did the image of a little girl whose two front teeth had not yet descended, also brought home the tragedy of a childhood cut short. In her personal account of covering the trial, Storer wrote: 'Another big moment came when a photo of a grinning eight-year-old, Charmaine West – the daughter of Fred's first wife Rena Costello (another victim) – was beamed onto the courtroom wall. Over it was placed a skull found at the Wests' former home at 25 Midland Road, Gloucester. There was an audible intake of breath when it was clear the two were an exact match.'

***

While the trial was underway, the jury sent a note to the judge requesting a tour of the Cromwell Street property. They wished to walk through the house to get a sense of its layout and size. That way, it would be easier to tell if one half of a married couple could do what had been done to the victims without the other person in the marriage knowing.

Justice Mantell agreed, and the arrangements were made, with the proposed tour falling on the day after Anne Marie had given her poignant, if harrowing, testimony.

The house had now become a symbol of the serial killing story that everybody loved to hate. Screens were erected around it to shield the jurors from the press who would be hovering, waiting to capture an image that would be beamed around the world. A small group of press members, however, would be allowed to enter the house as long as they shared their information with reporters from rival titles. For this privilege, they would have to win a draw. A journalist from the *Guardian* newspaper, Duncan Campbell, had his name drawn and, as press helicopters hovered overhead, he entered through the back of the house with the jurors and, like them, walked around in silence in what had since been dubbed 'The House of Horrors'.

Campbell shared his insights with all members of the press corps, who, in turn, could publish his findings. He said simply that, in his opinion, 'there was no way that Rose would not have been aware of what was going on in that house. It was very tiny and the noises that people must have heard would be very obvious.'

THE TRIAL

When it was time for the defence to present its case, few people expected Rose to take the stand at all. Her legal team had advised her to the contrary, but when the defence counsel rose to begin, she was the first witness called up. She had insisted on testifying, and Ferguson allowed her to regale those present with the stories of her difficult childhood.

Strangely, she never divulged being repeatedly raped by her father. Instead, she claimed to have been raped by a stranger before she met Fred.

'I suppose I fell for his lies,' she said.

Regarding Charmaine, she told the jury that 'the child started resisting [her] care', but she denied the abuse. Her rebuttal to the notion that the house was too small for murder and other violent crimes to go unnoticed was that Fred often sent her out to visit other men, thus giving him time to commit these ghastly crimes behind her back. When it came to the testimony of Caroline Owens, Rose waved it away with the glib comment, 'I just remember that it got out of hand,' before adding, 'I was as much a victim as Caroline was.'

When asked about wearing Lynda Gough's slippers, all she could say was, 'It wasn't me.' And with regard to Carole Ann Cooper, Lucy Partington, Therese Siegenthaler and Juanita Mott, she denied knowing any of them despite the circumstantial evidence.

As for Anne Marie's testimony, Rose admitted she had lost her temper with her, but said she 'thought the world of her'.

The last person she was asked about was Fred, and she insisted that she had no idea what kind of man he really was, telling the court, 'I couldn't live with a murderer.'

The prosecution relished the opportunity to go after Rose. They hadn't expected her to take the stand. Brian Leveson quickly proved that they were far more of a loving and connected couple than Rose had made out. He produced letters that Rose had signed 'your worshipping wife' and 'love you always'.

He also tore apart her story about speaking to Heather on the phone, which was obviously impossible since she was buried under the patio at the time. Rose was forced to backtrack, claiming that it was a 'bad line' and that she had thought it was Heather but it could have been someone else impersonating her.

As with any accused who takes the stand, Rose had the intense gaze of the entire courtroom fixed on her every move, searching for clues in her demeanour. In the press, she was described by words like 'unattractive', 'matronly' and 'stroppy'. One reporter wrote there was 'something very strange about the upper part of her face'.

Meaningless mistakes, like getting her own age wrong by a year, did not help her case, and neither did her attempts to use phrases that were not a natural fit for the way she normally spoke.

At one point, when Rose said, 'Sir, as I should like to emphasise,' the reporters called her a bumpkin. When she shed a few tears, they were deemed fake and rehearsed, and after Rose left the stand, the defence asked to have the tapes of Fred's interviews with the police played in court. The court now heard the voice of the deceased man who sat at the heart of the case with his wife he was trying to exonerate. But his testimony was unreliable and much of it was 'a sick fantasy', according to Howard Sounes, who was present in court.

In one particularly revealing exchange on tape, when Detective Savage put it to Fred that his victims had gone through hell, he seemed to be offended by that and replied, 'No, no one went through hell. Enjoyment turned to disaster.'

The prosecution was allowed to rebut Fred's testimony, so they called a woman called Janet Leach up to the stand.

She had been assigned as the 'appropriate adult' in Fred's case. In England and Wales, this term refers to an adult who accompanies a child under eighteen, or a vulnerable adult, whenever the person is going to be questioned by the police or other entities within the criminal justice system.

In Fred's case, Leach had been appointed because of his perceived low intelligence, and during his time in prison, Leach became a confidante to Fred and also developed an unhealthy bond with him after they had spent upwards of four hundred hours in one another's company.

She testified that Fred had revealed to her how Rose was indeed involved in the murders but that he had lied to the police by claiming he had acted alone.

This strengthened the prosecution's case but there was another twist to come.

Under cross-examination, Leach suddenly turned pale and looked as if she was about to pass out. Court was adjourned and she was rushed off to hospital. The reason soon became clear. She had sold the rights to a book about the case for £12,500, even though she had earlier denied under oath that she was receiving any payments for her story.

When she returned to court in a wheelchair a week later, it was put to her that she had lied and that she had thrown the case into jeopardy. It was a very strange episode of the trial. Leach seemed to be a completely different person after her reputation had been so shattered. The judge reflected on what had happened but ultimately decided to continue with the trial and let the jury come to its own conclusions about her testimony, which revealed how the married couple had worked in unison to commit their heinous crimes.

Seven weeks had passed with hundreds gathering each day in the crisp winter air at the courthouse buildings. From legal professionals to curious onlookers to broken family members of the deceased, a steady stream of people had made their way up the short stairwell outside and entered through the glass doors surrounded by the typical 1970s stone-in-cement facade.

On the final day, by the time both the prosecution and defence arrived in court holding lengthy print-outs of their closing statements, everyone had spent countless hours reeling from the details to which they'd been exposed.

For some, it had dragged them out of the numb pain of two decades of a missing child and into the dark world of the woman who was likely the last of two people to ever see them.

One such person was Alison Chambers's mother, Sue, who had travelled from Swansea with her husband to hear the verdict. She described to a journalist how the last time she had seen Alison was for a cup of tea at a hotel when Alison had left the family home and was fending for herself with no fixed address.

Over the many years since that day, she had missed her daughter very deeply but believed she was living her life somewhere and had a right to do so. Even when the gruesome news item had come on television in February the year before the trial, showing how some bones had been found in a garden in Gloucester, she still did not make the connection.

And here she was, nearly two years later, hollowed out by looking into the face of the woman accused of being an accomplice to rape, torture and murder.

She sat with her eyes peeled as Ferguson stood up to make his closing statement on Rose's behalf.

Ferguson, whose years in politics made him no stranger to giving rousing speeches, relied on the technicality of circumstantial evidence not being enough for a conviction.

Saddled with defending one of the most sadistic and hated women in England's modern history, he stuck to his guns and said, 'There is no forensic evidence to associate this defendant with these deaths, there is no eyewitness, no confession.'

He then went about listing the many other dark deeds of Rosemary West, including assault, cruelty to children, even rape, but these, he asserted, did not prove she had murdered.

'There is speculation, yes, opportunity perhaps, but proof no, and you cannot convict without proof,' Ferguson told the jury of seven men and four women at the Crown Court.

He also tried to squash the theory that Fred had tried to cover for Rose. '[He is] not the stuff that martyrs are made of,' said Ferguson, adding that Fred was 'devoid of compassion, consumed with sexual lust, and a sadistic killer ... [he] was the very epitome of evil'.

But, for prosecutor Brian Leveson and those who had gathered in the courtroom for so many weeks as one macabre story after another came to the fore, that exact description of Fred fitted Rosemary just as neatly.

In his closing arguments, he told the jury, 'We have travelled to a place which plumbs the depth of human depravity. The Wests were the perfect companions and did it together. On that basis, you can be sure that the allegations are proved.'

He described Rose as the 'strategist' and 'dominant partner' of the two, and added, 'The "evidence" that Rosemary West knew nothing is not worthy of belief.'

Now all held their breath to see which of these opposing views had captured the imagination of the jury.

***

The verdicts were delivered over two days. Rose was first convicted of murdering little Charmaine West when she was seventeen and the child, stoic and refusing to cry when beaten daily, was only eight. She was also convicted of killing Heather West, her own daughter of sixteen, who had just completed high school and was wanting to escape the traumas of the family home.

On that same day came the verdict regarding Shirley Robinson and her unborn child. Rose had committed murder most foul, cold-bloodedly removing anyone in her domestic set-up who was not to her liking.

Now there were seven counts still to work through, and a voice came over the intercom asking everyone involved in the trial to return to court three. The court filled up in an instant, and at exactly eight minutes to one, on this final day of the trial, the last seven verdicts were delivered.

The names of the dead, said for one last time in the courtroom, were now imbued at the very least with some justice: Lynda Gough aged 19, Carole Ann Cooper aged 15, Lucy Partington aged 21, Therese Siegenthaler aged 21, Shirley Hubbard aged 15, Juanita Mott aged 18 and Alison Chambers aged 19.

Seven times over, the word 'guilty' was repeated. The public gallery erupted in cheers, while Rose stood still with a stony face, staring through her big glasses perched on her chubby face. Her inscrutable reaction stood in sharp contrast to that of her stepdaughter, Anne Marie, who had provided a damning testimony in her soft voice to the shocked ears of the world and who now collapsed in the public gallery.

Justice Mantell said, 'Rosemary Pauline West, on each of the 10 counts of which you have been unanimously convicted by the jury, the sentence is one of life imprisonment. If attention is paid to what I think, you will never be released. Take her down.'

He then turned to the jury and said, 'You will not have had a more important job to do in your lives. I am fully aware of the great sacrifice each one of you has made.'

He also praised Ferguson and Leveson for conducting the trial 'without rancour or ill-temper' and said their closing addresses were 'two fine speeches'.

Leveson, he said, had been more 'analytical'. Ferguson, for his part, had 'used a broader brush to make his strokes – the difference between a Canaletto and a Van Gogh, you may say'.

Detective Superintendent John Bennett, who had led the investigation that had finally come to fruition in the halls of justice, said, 'It is quite clear that Mrs West must be a psychopath. She and Frederick were a perfect pair for each other.'

On this final day of the trial, when the world sat glued to televisions, radios and newspapers, Rosemary West's name would become synonymous with being Britain's most infamous female serial killer. But for the bereft families, the machinations of the criminal justice system had done little to take away the pain of knowing how their loved ones had died – and the bloody hands behind those acts.

As Alison's mother Sue so gently put it to a journalist covering the trial, 'People say at least you know where Alison now is. But I wanted to know where she was alive. Not where she was dead.'

18

Imprisonment Takes Many Forms

Rose West had spent her childhood in the uber-controlled environment created by her parents. When she left home at sixteen, she constructed a new world in which she went unchallenged, using verbal, sexual, physical and mental abuse and violence to control those in her homestead. Now here she was, as a middle-aged woman, living under lock and key in a prison cell. A strict set of rules and regulations would at first define every aspect of her institutionalised world. And, most importantly, no longer would she be able to act out her depraved fantasies on hapless victims from within and outside her own family.

But for her surviving children, the dismantling of homelife at 25 Cromwell Street barely marked a moment of liberation. A violent upbringing, discovering their parents' heinous crimes, and the shame of living with the West name held each child in psychological captivity.

When Rose began her sentence at the imposing Category B prison called HMP Durham, she was 42 years old. By then, Mae and Stephen were in their early twenties, Barry, Tara and Louise were teenagers, and Lucyanna and Rosemary Junior were still under the age of ten. Anne Marie by then was 31, and every single one of them, to varying degrees, would battle to live a life not haunted by their past.

The imposing Georgian structure of Rose's new 'home' in the eastern part of Durham dated back to the early 1800s and had capacity for 980 prisoners. It included a high-security wing to house 120 female prisoners in their own section behind the drab, brick walls, and it was here where Rose's schedule could not be further away from a life she had once lived: working out of Mandy's room or waiting for Fred to get home from work so they could cruise the streets for victims.

With all the media hype around her case, she likely expected to be the most 'famous' prisoner confined between those walls, but this would not be the case. HMP Durham was also home to one of Britain's most notorious prisoners ever: Myra Hindley. She was an English serial killer who, along with her partner Ian Brady, murdered five children between 1963 and 1965. The crimes, which came to be known as the Moors Murders, shocked the nation. Hindley was known to lure boys and girls to secluded spots before Brady would sexually assault and kill them. On more than one occasion, Hindley participated in the assaults. After a reign of terror that lasted years, the pair were arrested in 1965 after they had tried to implicate Hindley's teen brother-in-law. They had done this by making him watch as they killed someone with an axe. After he turned them in to the police, Brady and Hindley were both sentenced to life in prison.

And so, by the time Rose West was led through the heavy doors of HMP Durham late in 1995, Myra Hindley had already been incarcerated since the age of 23 and was a dab hand at working the prison system.

But shortly before Rose's arrival, Hindley had fractured her femur while exercising in the prison yard on 17 April. She had been in agony for four days before she was moved to the prison hospital.

As is customary with new lifers, Rose began her sentence in the prison with a physical and psychological examination. This meant she was also in the hospital section of the prison, and it did not take long before the two infamous murderers were drawn to one another.

As Rose adjusted to her new surroundings, she struck up a friendship with Hindley. She told her former solicitor Leo Goatley, 'Yeah, Myra, she's all right, we get on, I want to see how it goes.' Rose was impressed that Hindley had been trying to better herself in prison by taking a number of courses through the Open University. According to Goatley, Rose West was 'impressed by Hindley's knowledge and ability'.

A friendship between Britain's two most notorious female serial killers was manna from heaven for the tabloid newspapers that had made millions from reporting on the House of Horrors case and were in no mood for that to come to an end.

Rumours spread quickly that the friendship had developed into a romance while the women were locked up together. But despite the fevered dreams of journalists and editors, the relationship didn't last very long at all, and the next time Goatley visited Rose to discuss her appeal, she told him, 'You have to watch Hindley, mind. She is very manipulative. You don't realise it, but she gets you doing stuff for her. Oh, she's clever, all right. She's flippin' dangerous, that one. She ain't going to take me for a c**t again.'

For the children, their mother describing another woman as being dangerous might have redefined the word irony.

In February 2024, on the thirtieth anniversary of the grim discoveries at the family house, journalist Stephen Wright, who had reported on the case for the *Daily Mail*, made a keen observation: 'Many books have been written about the West case and countless TV documentaries made. All have focused largely on the killers and those they slaughtered. But there is another category of victim whose stories have not been reported so widely.'

These, he added, are the West children, 'brought up in the most depraved and dysfunctional family imaginable'.

Anne Marie was thirty years old when Rose was incarcerated, and her repeated rapes, beginning at age eight and ending at age fifteen when she finally fled after being impregnated by her father, still haunted her. These were now compounded by the brutal truth of hearing that her mother Rena and two half-sisters, Heather and Charmaine, had all been murdered and dismembered several years before and at different times.

She went on to write her biography *Out of the Shadows*, in which she detailed her life in the same gentle but candid way in which she had recounted it in the witness stand and in a documentary a few years later.

As journalist Stephen Wright described it thirty years later, 'Nobody who heard her harrowing evidence against her stepmother Rose will ever forget it.' And certainly, Wright was referring not only to the gobsmacking cruelty of the content, but the soft and vulnerable way in which it was shared so authentically.

Anne Marie had been so traumatised by the court case and giving testimony that she attempted to kill herself barely two weeks after the trial was over by throwing herself into the River Severn. She survived that attempt and tried to rebuild her life but limped through the next few years, haunted by her past and the loss of her family. In 1999, she couldn't take it any longer and tried again to end it all. She was swept half a mile down the River Severn and was dragged by firemen from the reeds of the riverbed, blue and close to death.

She was quoted in the media delivering words that summed up her life: 'People say I am lucky to have survived, but I wish

I had died. I can still taste the fear. Still feel the pain. It's like going back to being a child again.'

It would take Anne Marie more than a decade to finally break the spell of feeling compelled to love and maintain some sort of connection with the woman who had tortured and raped her and murdered those she loved. Her complicated feelings for her stepmother, so evident back at the trial in 1994, would fuel her for years until eventually, in 2012, she spoke to her for the very last time.

That's how long it took for the reality to sink in: Rose was never going to do justice to the living or the dead and come clean about what she had done. With this awareness that Rose would take her secrets to the grave, Anne Marie decided the best choice for her mental health was, finally, to let go.

This had been Anne Marie's own decision, but for Marian Partington, the bereft sister of Lucy, her journey of reaching out to Rose as an act of forgiveness fell on deaf ears. Marian had responded to the brutal murder of her sister by starting The Forgiveness Project, a not-for-profit organisation that shares inspirational stories from survivors and perpetrators who have rebuilt their lives.

To explain why she had chosen this road after learning of her sister's cruel ending, she had written a piece in which she explained her epiphany during the trial. 'When I saw Rosemary West sitting there, it was almost impossible to match her expressionless face with the endless graphic details of sexual depravities and brutality. But then I heard her voice on tape, shouting, swearing and full of rage, and I began to have some insight into her mind ... Her story seems to be about the impoverishment of a soul that knew no other way to live than through terrible cruelty.'

In 2011, she reached out to the imprisoned Rose via a letter, explaining the road she had travelled to reach a place of forgiveness. This, she had hoped, would be met with some graciousness on the part of the woman who had tortured and killed her sister.

On receiving the letter, Rose had refused to write back.

Instead, she responded by asking the prison authorities to tell Marian to never write to her again.

***

The anguish of adults whose lives had been so vastly damaged by growing up at 25 Cromwell Street stood in sharp contrast to the life her mother was living in prison, a life that was only getting more comfortable as the years went by.

In 2001, the prison where she lived was hailed as a model for rehabilitation, integration and its low levels of violence. Rose enrolled in a hairdressing and beauty course and began cutting fellow inmates' hair.

The following year, she received a letter from a young man named Dave Glover. He was a musician in his mid-thirties who had joined well-known seventies rock band Slade in their later years. Flattered to receive a letter from a rock star, she responded in kind and soon started receiving letters from him every other day.

Through their correspondence, a romance of sorts began, and news soon spread that the two were engaged and would be married in the chapel at the prison. The media machine spun into action with glee. The scrutiny was so intense that a few days later, the engagement was unceremoniously called off and correspondence between the two dried up. Band leader David Hill announced that he was 'horrified' and that he was glad to see the back of a man who would stoop so low as to propose to notorious serial murderer Rose West.

'He's a nice bloke and all that, but this is just totally sick,' he said.

Around the same time as Rose's doomed love affair, Rosemary's eldest son Stephen was struggling to build his own healthy relationships. He tried for years to live down the West name, with some success, but the trauma of his childhood stalked him. Throughout his twenties, he suffered from post-traumatic stress disorder but never sought treatment. Working as an electrician, he also had more than one door slam in his face when it dawned on customers that this was Fred West's son, with a strong family resemblance to boot, standing before them. In fact, Anne Marie, too, had reportedly lost her job as a cook in a school canteen when the children at the school joined the dots.

These moments of ostracisation for the offspring of Fred and Rosemary saw them treated as pariahs rather than survivors of what was one of the most violent households in modern British history.

In 2004, when he was 31, Stephen impregnated a fourteen-year-old girl. All of a sudden, the long shadow of his childhood was cast onto his adulthood, especially when he sought someone to perform a backstreet abortion. This resulted in his arrest, and he was convicted of having sex with an underage girl and sentenced to nine months in jail.

The court case burst open the trauma of Stephen's childhood, which brought more compassion than shame to the situation. Because Stephen was deemed to have the emotional maturity of a teenager, and because he had not groomed the teenager, who had willingly taken part in the act, the court took mercy on him. The judge said it was 'quite clear' the girl felt she was in love with him that he should have realised the relationship was wrong.

It prompted Stephen to reflect on the man who had raised him, with him saying, 'Perhaps there is a little of my father in me.'

Stephen cut ties with Rose five years into her jail sentence after she spewed hatred towards him in a phone call, saying she wished he'd died when he was born.

But in the end, his time in jail turned out to be a blessing. He was able to access therapy, deal at least to some extent with his past, and turn his life around. Years later, he would marry and have children of his own.

Back in prison, the era of success at HMP Durham began to shift to something darker, and by 2004, the prison was facing accusations of overcrowding as well as a lack of educational and work opportunities for the inmates. In 2005, all the female prisoners of HMP Durham were moved, and Rosemary found herself transferred into unfamiliar surroundings at HMP Low Newton, three miles north.

For the next decade, Rose West would call Low Newton her home, and it was one in which she sought and received a comfortable routine in a relatively well-resourced prison. It hardly seemed a fitting punishment for the slate of crimes she had committed.

But for other family members, the hurdles of the past sometimes seemed impossible to overcome.

In 2006, Fred's first rape victim, his younger sister Kitty, passed away. Amidst all the suffering in Fred's family, Kitty's story was largely forgotten. She carried with her years of pain and the guilt of knowing that, had she pressed charges all those years ago, maybe things could have been different. Her husband told journalist Howard Sounes in no uncertain terms that Fred was 'what killed my wife'. In his book, Sounes added, 'I knew what he meant. The publicity of her brother's murder case, the attention of the police and people like me, asking difficult, intimate questions. There was pain and suffering in the family long before Fred's murders were uncovered.'

It was around this time that Mae West finally freed herself from any contact with Rose. For the past ten years, she had stayed in contact with the mother who had put her through hell and perhaps, she believed, might change once incarcerated.

That hope died around 2006 when Mae received a note from Rose that said, 'It's best if I leave you to it.' Despite all that had happened, it was now the mother cutting contact with the daughter, and Mae would tell a local journalist, 'She no longer wanted to see me or communicate with me.'

Mae went on to build as healthy and functional a life as possible, and her survival despite the odds was captured in her memoir entitled *Love as Always, Mum xxx*, so called because of how Rosemary would sign off her letters from prison. The book was well received as a no-holds-barred take on surviving trauma and the psychological impact of abuse.

Meantime, with family members still seeking solace and meaning in the aftermath of this depraved story, Rose was content in her new surroundings at HMP Low Newton, a prison exclusively for women and young offenders. Her prison life had been dramatically upgraded.

Now she found herself living in her own en suite cell, complete with curtains at the window, a fluffy rug on the floor, a coffee machine, television and radio. She regularly went to the gym, took yoga classes a few times a week and spent her days baking cakes, listening to radio soap opera *The Archers*, and obsessing over *Dancing on Ice* on television.

Contrast these domestic scenes behind the walls of a physical prison with the mental incarceration of Barry West, the second and last son born to Rosemary and Fred.

Barry was only fourteen when his parents were arrested and, along with four of his siblings, had been taken into care before that, after the case of his sister Louise's assault had caught the attention of the authorities.

Though life at home had been brutal, the rupture of all that followed augmented his fate as someone who would not cope.

Haunted by nightmares and the ghosts of his past, he never found peace. He always carried with him the memory of Heather being savagely beaten by their parents when she returned home late one night. In his mind as a little boy of seven, he convinced himself that that was the night she was killed. The forensic evidence showed that Heather was killed on a morning, but this enduring memory that Barry carried with him was one of many such brutal attacks by his parents on the children in the house, and, traumatised by Heather's death, he likely fused those incidents in his mind.

Barry developed an opioid and heroin addiction around 2002 as a way of blotting out his memories, and it held him in a grip until the end of life from an overdose at the age of forty during the Covid pandemic. Before his death on 28 August in 2020, Barry admitted feeling abandoned by the health services. He was found slumped over a table by his support worker at the assisted living facility in Maidstone, after taking an overdose of medication for chronic pain. When his 'next of kin' were informed, it included four grown women who were once his little sisters and playmates at the House of Horrors. Louise, Tara, Lucyanna and Rosemary Junior, who had been taken in by social services all those years ago alongside Barry, had managed to carve out balanced lives for themselves, or at the very least, anonymous lives not marked by the name of Fred and Rosemary West. One way or another, despite everything, they had survived. But for Barry, it had all proven too much.

This was yet another scene of tragedy that Rose had left in the wake of her decades as a monstrous killer. And here she was, living an institutionalised but very comfortable life.

The slight fifteen-year-old with a pixie-like face who had once been wooed at a bus stop by Fred West was now an obese jailbird who baked frequently and whose weight had ballooned to over eighteen stone. Classified as 'dangerously overweight', she was told by the medical personnel at the prison that she would die if she didn't change her life.

There was another and more immediate danger lurking, however.

In July of 2019, the sadistic serial killer Joanna Dennehy, aged 37, was moved to Low Newton prison. An unbridled psychopath who had gone on a ten-day killing spree in 2013, she had left three men dead and two critically injured.

After the death of Myra Hindley in 2002, Rose West and Joanna Dennehy were the only two women in England who were serving full life sentences for murder. With Low Newton being the highest security prison for women in the country, the authorities were in no doubt where Dennehy belonged. But as soon as she arrived in Low Newton, she was overheard saying to another prisoner, 'I'll kill that bitch.'

Her target was Rose West, and with the prison authorities taking her threat at face value, they moved the now-elderly Rose, no longer considered a flight risk, to New Hall jail in Wakefield, West Yorkshire.

Rose, who had callously beaten and butchered so many people and who had remained poker-faced when convicted, now showed extreme emotion. She reportedly wept only when informed she would be walking away from the prison where she had spent ten of the best years of her life, and she arrived at her new place of incarceration just as the Covid pandemic began to grip the world.

Little is known about Rose's life in what will likely be the final institution to house her, but one thing seems certain: she will not divulge any details of the serial killings before she dies.

Like Fred, this could be one of her most selfish acts ever. When he hanged himself on New Year's Day in 1995, he had mentioned the existence of scores of other victims who would never be found. Though he was prone to massive hyperbole, it rings true for such a bloody-minded man. For the family of Mary Bastholm, this whole dark saga of mystery, loss, pain and vague glimmers of hope was reignited in 2021. Fred had, after all, confessed to her murder to more than one person, though never to the authorities.

A TV crew making a documentary about the West case took a cadaver dog into the Clean Plate cafe where she had worked. The dog reacted to a particular spot in the basement while a radar image appeared to show what some thought was Mary's clothing.

This was enough for the police to shut down the cafe and a search, reminiscent of the one at Cromwell Street all those years ago, began.

The sudden awakening of the story came as a shock to Mae. She longed for Mary's family to find closure, but in equal measure, it triggered the horrors of the life she once lived.

Despite their best attempts, the authorities found nothing, and so it was that Mary's loved ones were hurled headlong back into the agony of not knowing what had become of their daughter.

She had disappeared before Rose and Fred had met, but if he was her killer, it foreshadowed the modus operandi that the monstrous couple would go on to 'perfect'.

Today, Heather West would be in her early fifties. Charmaine would be nearing retirement age, and all the young women whose names were read out in that cold courtroom back in 1994 as victims of murder would have led full and interesting lives. Instead, they were used and then discarded for the pleasure of Rosemary West and her husband.

The name Rose West will forever be etched in history as one of the most sadistic and notorious serial killers ever born on British soil.

Perhaps finally even she felt the burden of carrying it around: in December 2020, she paid £36 to change her name by deed poll to Jennifer Jones.

Like the daughter she killed, she finally shed the West name.

In the peaceful gardens of St Michael's Church in Tintern Parva, Wales, on a tombstone adorned by an angel carved in stone and a loving inscription by her siblings, it simply says 'Heather'.

Bibliography

Amis, Martin, *Guardian*, 2000, 'When darkness met light'
https://www.theguardian.com/theguardian/2000/may/11/features11.g2

Attwood, Shaun, *Shaun Attwood Podcast*
https://youtu.be/VegjioGJnKw?si=qSVb2oGl_UCzZKhq&t=4040

Bardsley, Marilyn, Crime Library, 'Fred & Rose West'
https://www.crimelibrary.org/serial_killers/weird/west/endgame_7.html

BBC, '1995: Life sentence for Rosemary West'
http://news.bbc.co.uk/onthisday/hi/dates/stories/november/22/newsid_2549000/2549073.stm

BBC, 2021, 'The 12 victims of Fred and Rosemary West'
https://www.bbc.com/news/uk-england-gloucestershire-57182844

'BEHIND CLOSED DOORS: Anne Marie West'
https://www.youtube.com/watch?v=g6moQKEzZ9s

Bennett, Will, *Independent*, 1995, 'Daughter "was abused from age of 8"' https://www.independent.co.uk/news/daughter-was-abused-from-age-of-8-1578265.html

Bennett, Will, *Independent*, 1995, 'Rosemary West tells of Fred and sex'
https://www.independent.co.uk/news/rosemary-west-tells-of-fred-and-sex-1580231.html

Bennett, Will, *Independent*, 1995, 'Step-daughter Charmaine was first to die'
https://www.independent.co.uk/news/stepdaughter-charmaine-was-first-to-die-1583071.html

Bennett, Will, *Independent*, 1995, 'THE BODIES: Litany of sadness: the lives of West's twelve female victims'
https://www.independent.co.uk/news/uk/the-bodies-litany-of-sadness-the-lives-of-west-s-twelve-female-victims-1566334.html

Bulmer, Joe, 2017, 'Who is Rose West? – The Devon born serial killer who is seriously ill'
https://www.devonlive.com/news/devon-news/who-rose-west-devon-born-769292

Burn, Gordon, *Happy Like Murderers* (Faber & Faber, 2011)

Campbell, Duncan, and Donegan, Lawrence, *Guardian*, 1995, 'You will never be released'
https://www.newspapers.com/article/the-guardian-fred-west/37301322/

Carter Woodrow, Jane, *Rose West: The Making of a Monster* (Hodder & Stoughton, 2021)

Cassidy, Peter, *Glasgow Live*, 'How the Gorbals Cumbie chased Fred West out of town – the history of Glasgow's street gangs'
https://www.glasgowlive.co.uk/news/history/gangs-gorbals-cumbie-fred-west-12266308

Channel 5, *The Clues that Caught the Killer Fred & Rose*
https://www.channel5.com/show/the-clues-that-caught-the-killer-fred-rose-west

Crime + Investigation, 'Fred West pure evil?'
   https://www.crimeandinvestigation.co.uk/crime-files/fred-west
Crime + Investigation, 'The Trial'
   https://www.crimeandinvestigation.co.uk/crime-files/
   rosemary-west/trial
Dalrymple, Theodore, *City Journal*, 1996, 'A Horror Story'
   https://www.city-journal.org/article/a-horror-story
Davies, Nicola, 'Making of a Monster: Rose West'
   https://healthpsychologyconsultancy.wordpress.com/
   2012/02/23/making-of-a-monster-rose-west/
Forgiveness Project, The, 'Our Purpose'
   https://www.theforgivenessproject.com/stories-library/
   marian-partington/
Freeman, James, *Herald*, 1995, 'Life and death of a good mother'
   https://www.heraldscotland.com/news/12062252.life-and-
   death-of-a-good-mother/
Gerrard, Nicci, *Observer*, 1999, '"I can still taste the fear"'
   https://www.theguardian.com/theobserver/1999/nov/21/
   featuresreview.review4
Goatley, Leo, *Understanding Fred and Rose West: Noose, Lamella and the Gilded Cage* (The Book Guild, 2019)
Goodkind, Summer, *Mail Online*, 2024, 'Daughter of serial killers Fred and Rose West reveals the awful secret she carries around with her everyday – and the letter her evil mother wrote to her from prison'
   https://www.dailymail.co.uk/news/article-13123703/fred-
   rose-west-daughter-letter-prison-serial-killers.html
Gloucestershire Police Archives, 'Police Stations Gloucester'
   https://gloucestershirepolicearchives.org.uk/content/new-
   contributions/police-stations-gloucester
   https://www.theforgivenessproject.com/our-purpose/
Gould, Paul, UPI, 1995, 'Judge sums up UK "horrors" murder trial

https://www.upi.com/Archives/1995/11/16/Judge-sums-up-UK-horrors-murder-trial/4423816498000/

Gould, Paul, UPI, 1995, 'The defense in the serial murder trial of Rosemary …'
https://www.upi.com/Archives/1995/11/15/The-defense-in-the-serial-murder-trial-of-Rosemary/1913816411600/

Hardy, Frances, *Mail Online*, 2018, 'How I survived growing up in the House of Horrors – by Fred and Rose West's daughter'
https://www.dailymail.co.uk/news/article-6120107/How-survived-growing-House-Horrors-Fred-Rose-Wests-daughter.html

Herald, 1995, 'Jury hears killer's voice describe how victims were strangled, dismembered, and buried. Monologue of murder'
https://www.heraldscotland.com/news/12063755.jury-hears-killers-voice-describe-how-victims-were-strangled-dismembered-and-buried-monologue-of-murder/

Herald, 1997, 'Brother of Fred West "knew about murders"'
https://www.heraldscotland.com/news/12327412.brother-of-fred-west-knew-about-murders/

Historic UK, 'The year that was … 1953'
https://www.historic-uk.com/CultureUK/The-year-that-was-1953/

Hughes, Janet, *Gloucestershire Live*, 2023, 'Sky TV documentary Fred West: The Glasgow Girls asks if serial killer could have been stopped before Gloucester murders'
https://www.gloucestershirelive.co.uk/news/gloucester-news/sky-tv-documentary-fred-west-8125320

Independent, 1995, 'Couple told victim she would be buried'
https://www.independent.co.uk/news/couple-told-victim-she-would-be-buried-1576968.html

Irish Times, 1996, 'Inquiry completed into claim that police used West house as brothel' https://www.irishtimes.com/news/inquiry-completed-into-claim-that-police-used-west-house-as-brothel-1.60815

IWC Media, 'Fred West: The Glasgow Girls'
https://iwcmedia.co.uk/shows/fred-west-the-glasgow-girls

Kelly, Amanda, *Independent*, 1998, 'I survived Fred and Rose West'
https://www.independent.co.uk/arts-entertainment/i-survived-fred-and-rose-west-1196933.html

Kindon, Frances, *Mirror*, 2024, 'Fred and Rose West's children – who are they and what happened to them?'
https://www.mirror.co.uk/news/uk-news/fred-rose-wests-children-who-32197711

Knight, Adam, *Hereford Times*, 2014, 'Fred West's brother denies incest claims'
https://www.herefordtimes.com/news/11587578.Fred_West_s_brother_denies_incest_claims/

Lavender, Jane, *Daily Record*, 2019, 'Mistake serial killer Rose West made in court that turned husband Fred against her'
https://www.dailyrecord.co.uk/news/uk-world-news/mistake-serial-killer-rose-west-18331736

Lavender, Jane, *Mirror*, 2020, 'Fred West turned against wife Rose after her brutal reaction to him in court'

MailOnline, 2004, 'Fred West's son jailed for under-age sex'
https://www.dailymail.co.uk/news/article-329497/Fred-Wests-son-jailed-age-sex.html

Meares, Richard, *Daily News*, 1995
https://news.google.com/newspapers?nid=1241&dat=19951005&id=MkZTAAAAIBAJ&pg=5428,1631027&hl=en

MGH Center for Women's Mental Health, 2021, 'Essential Reads: Guidelines for the Use of Electroconvulsive Therapy During Pregnancy' https://womensmentalhealth.org/posts/ect-pregnancy/

Midlands Partnership University, 'Schizophrenia'
https://www.mpft.nhs.uk/services/military-mental-health-service/mental-health-problems/schizophrenia

Morbid, Episode 567: 'Fred & Rose West (Part 4)' (transcription) https://www.happyscribe.com/public/morbid/episode-567-fred-rose-west-part-4

Morris-Grant, Brianna, ABC NEWS, 2024, 'Fred and Rose West claimed the lives of 12 young women and girls. Thirty years on, some questions remain unanswered' https://www.abc.net.au/news/2024-03-10/fred-rose-west-victims-anniversary/103453858

Nelson, Sara C., *Huffpost*, 2018, 'Serial Killer Fred West "Murdered A Three-Year-Old With An Ice Cream Van"' https://www.huffingtonpost.co.uk/entry/serial-killer-fred-west-murdered-a-three-year-old-by-running-him-down-with-an-ice-cream-van_uk_5b714db6e4b0530743cb5687

Nicholson, Kate, *Express*, 1999,
https://www.express.co.uk/news/uk/1189669/fred-west-rose-west-serial-killers-sister-abuse-eventual-death-gloucester-murders-spt

Norris, Phil, *Gloucestershire Live*, 2019, 'Solicitor who represented Rose West set to reveal all in new book about Cromwell Street killer'
https://www.gloucestershirelive.co.uk/news/gloucester-news/rose-wests-solicitor-reveal-understanding-3270269

Norris, Phil, *Gloucestershire Live*, 2021, 'House of Horrors timeline: Day-by-day investigation into
Cromwell Street killers Fred and Rose West'
https://www.gloucestershirelive.co.uk/news/gloucester-news/house-horrors-timeline-day-day-2567483

Old Ledbury, 'Youth Club, 13 The Southend'
http://www.old-ledbury.co.uk/southendyouthclub.htm

O'Sullivan, Kyle, *Mirror*, 2021, 'How Rose West became monster in childhood – brutal therapy in womb and father's sexual abuse' https://www.mirror.co.uk/tv/tv-news/how-rose-west-became-monster-23745131

Paediatrics & Child Health, 2004, 'Depression in pregnant women and mothers: How children are affected'
https://www.ncbi.nlm.nih.gov/pmc/articles/PMC2724170/
https://www.mirror.co.uk/tv/tv-news/fred-west-turned-against-wife-22717935

Ridler, Faith, *MailOnline*, 2021, 'Fred and Rose West's son, 40, who saw serial killer parents beat his sister to death when he was just seven died of overdose after telling doctor life was "not worth living", inquest hears'
https://www.dailymail.co.uk/news/article-9474007/Fred-Rose-Wests-son-40-died-painkiller-overdose-inquest-hears.html

'ROSE WEST – THE UNPRINTED INTERVIEW'
https://neil-paton.tripod.com/inter.htm

Sillem, Tanya, and Wandless, Paul, *Independent*, 1995, 'More questions than answers'
https://www.independent.co.uk/news/uk/more-questions-than-answers-1583744.html

Sounes, Howard, *Fred & Rose: The Full Story of Fred and Rose West and the Gloucester House of Horrors* (Sphere, 2019)

Sounes, Howard, *Unheard: The Fred and Rose West Tapes* podcast

Storer, Jackie, BBC, 2005
http://news.bbc.co.uk/2/hi/uk_news/4439184.stm

Styles, Ruth, *MailOnline*, 2014, '"I still feel guilty about what happened to the others": Nanny who was raped by serial killers Fred and Rose West says she wishes she had done more to have them jailed'
https://www.dailymail.co.uk/femail/article-2737548/Nanny-raped-serial-killers-Fred-Rose-West-says-wishes-jailed.html

This Morning, 2021, 'New Evidence in Fred West Murder Case Over 50 Years On Could Find Missing Girl'
https://www.youtube.com/watch?v=zs22mVxOM44

Thompson, Danny, *Coventry Telegraph*, 2021, 'Fred West, the infamous serial killer secretly cremated in Coventry'
https://www.coventrytelegraph.net/news/coventry-news/fred-west-infamous-serial-killer-20584080

Wansell, Geoffrey, *An Evil Love: The Life and Crimes of Fred West* (John Blake, 2022)

West, Anne Marie, *Out of the Shadows* (Simon & Schuster, 1995)

West, Mae, *Love as Always, Mum xxx: The true and terrible story of surviving a childhood with Fred and West* (Seven Dials, 2019)

Wings, 'Intrafamilial sexual abuse or Incest'
https://www.wingsfound.org/resource/intrafamilial-abuse/

Wright, Stephen, *Mail Online*, 2024, 'What happened to Fred and Rosemary West's children'
https://www.dailymail.co.uk/news/article-13103789/what-happened-Fred-Rosemary-Wests-children-stephen-wright.html